GETTING STARTED WITH LEGO® TRAINS

GETTING STARTED WITH LEGO® TRAINS

JACOB H. MCKEE

NO STARCH
PRESS

SAN FRANCISCO

Printed in China

1 2 3 4 5 6 7 8 9 10 — 06   05   04   03

PUBLISHER: William Pollock
MANAGING EDITOR: Karol Jurado
COVER AND INTERIOR DESIGN AND COMPOSITION: Octopod Studios
COPYEDITOR: Andy Carroll

For information on translations or book distributors, please contact No Starch Press, Inc. directly:

No Starch Press, Inc.

555 De Haro Street, Suite 250, San Francisco, CA 94107

phone: 415-863-9900; fax: 415-863-9950; info@nostarch.com; http://www.nostarch.com

Library of Congress Cataloging-in-Publication Data

McKee, Jacob H.
        Getting started with LEGO (R) trains / Jacob H. McKee.
        p. cm.
        ISBN 1-59327-006-2 (pbk.)
          1.   Railroads - Models - Design and construction.   2.   LEGO toys.   I.   Title.
TF197.M43 2003
623.1'9--dc21

2003013302

ACKNOWLEDGMENTS

Let me start off by giving a very warm thanks to the LEGO fan community, without whom much of this book wouldn't have happened. In recent years, and even in recent months, the LEGO community has begun to produce more designs, books, events, magazines, and projects than I ever envisioned when I first joined this community.

Big thanks to James Mathis, Steve Barile, Dan Parker, and Jonathan Lopes for their help and support with this book. Special thanks to James Mathis; he and I have developed some wonderful LEGO Train models, working with fans around the world.

Kevin Clauge's LPub program (http://www.users.qwest.net/~kclague/LPub/) was a wonderful help to this book, and he cannot go without credit. Thanks, Kevin!

And lastly and most importantly, many thanks to my lovely wife, Donna. Without her support, excitement, and encouragement, this book wouldn't have happened.

PHOTO CREDITS

All photographs of actual trains (except the black and white reefer photograph on page 49) are used with the permission of Matt Van Hattem. All model photographs and renderings are used with the permission of Jacob H. KcKee. The black and white reefer photograph on page 49 is used with the permission of the Kansas State Historical Society.

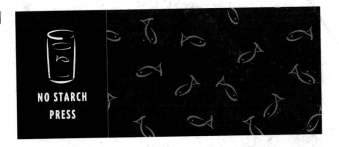

JOE NAGATA'S LEGO® MINDSTORMS IDEA BOOK

BY JOE NAGATA

More than 500,000 people own LEGO MINDSTORMS Robotics Invention System kits

Covers the MINDSTORMS Robotics Invention System 1.5 and can be used with all future kits

The LEGO MINDSTORMS Robotics Invention System from LEGO combines LEGO bricks with a programmable component, making it easy to create real working robots at home. This fun and easy guide to using LEGO MINDSTORMS shows how to build ten fascinating robots, and discusses the basic robotics principles needed to create variations. Step-by-step illustrated directions make the projects easy for users at all levels. Includes a four-color insert and creative ways to enjoy the robots that readers create. (Some projects require pieces not included with the MINDSTORMS kit.)

JOE NAGATA is a computer graphic artist living in Japan and the head of the Mindstorms Gallery (http://member.nifty.ne.jp/minstorms/).

April 2001, 300 pp.
$21.95 ($32.95 CDN)
ISBN 1-886411-40-9

You can find our books everywhere, or you can order directly from us:

PHONE:
800.420.7420 or +1 415.863.9900
MONDAY THROUGH FRIDAY
9AM TO 5PM (PST)

FAX:
+1 415.863.9950

EMAIL:
SALES@NOSTARCH.COM

WEB:
WWW.NOSTARCH.COM

MAIL:
NO STARCH PRESS, INC.
555 DE HARO STREET, SUITE 250
SAN FRANCISCO, CA 94107
USA

LINKS

Check out this book's website for more information on LEGO trains. At **http://www.bricksonthebrain.com/trains**, you'll find:

- Links to other LEGO Train websites
- Links to the www.LEGO.com trains website
- Information on starting your own local LEGO Train Club
- Links to additional LEGO Train building instructions from other LEGO enthusiasts
- Further information on building LEGO Trains
- Downloadable instructions
- Downloadable LEGO Train posters
- Discussions about LEGO Trains

...and much more!

Visit often as content will continue to grow!

BRIEF CONTENTS

CONTENTS IN DETAIL

PART ONE

PART TWO: PROJECTS

CHAPTER 7: TRACK LAYOUTS

APPENDIX A: RAILROAD TERMINOLOGY

APPENDIX B: WHERE TO BUY LEGO TRAINS

CHAPTER 1

INTRODUCTION

Since the first steam engine ran in the early 1800s, kids and adults around the world have been fascinated. Trains, then as now, hold a special appeal to many, and over the decades thousands of train models and toys have been created. Model railroads built by kids and adults alike have a long and rich history.

To this day, many of us love to set up model railroads and watch them run across our floors, through our basements, or on our detailed train layouts. Some of you may have tried your hand at model railroading with HO or N scale trains, but you may not have had much experience with LEGO Trains. You may have built other types of LEGO models, and perhaps some of them had some amount of movement or animation. But what makes LEGO Trains so fun is the fact that they all move at your command!

I often get asked why I build in "L-gauge"—LEGO Trains—instead of some other gauge, like HO, for instance. It's always a tough question to answer. Not because I don't have an answer, but rather because there are so many answers to give!

- Uncommon constraints: Model railroaders build their designs to a very specific scale, and everything is meant to look as lifelike as possible. All models are always exactly the same scale and match real-life prototypes (or versions). LEGO Trains, by comparison, are built with only LEGO elements, so the train designs are close approximations of the real-life design. Because of this difference, LEGO Trains require a whole new way of looking at the design process.

- Reusable materials: Most model railroading can be extremely expensive over time, since you have to continually purchase and repurchase expendable resources like paints, sheet plastic, hobby wood, and so on. But with LEGO, you can use and reuse parts over and over again. (Assuming, of course, you can bring yourself to take apart some of your creations!)

- Variations of scale and concepts: Because of the reusability and non-specific scale of LEGO Trains, it is possible to build all kinds of creations and train layouts. One week you can build 6-stud-wide hopper cars, and the next week 8-stud-wide circus trains!

All these reasons, and your own, create a terrific mix and an engaging, challenging, and fun design process.

In this book, we are going to dive into that design process and get you started with your own LEGO Trains. We are going to build a locomotive and a few different train cars. We will also look at track layouts, speed regulators,

6/8 Studs Wide

COMMON LEGO TRAIN WIDTHS ARE 6 STUDS AND 8 STUDS, THOUGH ALL OFFICIAL LEGO TRAIN MODELS ARE 6 WIDE. A FEW BUILDERS EVEN BUILD 12 OR 14' STUDS WIDE!

and more. Everything you need to know to get started with LEGO Trains!

A BRIEF HISTORY OF LEGO TRAINS

Before we start creating your future with LEGO Trains, let's take a look at the evolution of LEGO Trains since its early beginnings in 1965. In this year, LEGO released its first "train"—a push locomotive that ran on regular LEGO wheels and did not include track. This locomotive wasn't powered at all, and in 1966, this push train was replaced by a powered version.

The original LEGO Train track was plastic and was held together with special 2×8 plates. The gauge, or distance between the rails, was six studs (1.5 inches or 38 MM). Interestingly, the gauge was determined by the width of the wheels mounted on the ends of one 2×4 brick.

The powered trains have been going strong since 1966 and have included not one, but three separate systems of train tracks and sets, each defined by their voltage requirements.

- 4.5 VOLT (4.5V)
  The first powered LEGO Train was in the 4.5V range. This set used the standard LEGO motor, with power coming from batteries in a car directly behind the locomotive (motor). The trains

used track that was built with separate pieces of blue rail and white crossties. This line used hook-type couplers to join the cars, and later magnets. Over time, several improvements were made to the system, including gray rails, rather than blue, improvements to the magnets, and more.

This line was fairly small and didn't offer much opportunity for "real" model railroading.

- 12 VOLT (12V)
  Building on the success of the initial 4.5 volt line, a 12 volt line was introduced shortly after. Like Lionel trains, the 12v system used a "third rail" (a rail down the center of the track, which in this case was actually two smaller rails) to feed power to the motor, rather than using batteries. This third rail was available separately, which allowed older battery-powered layouts to be upgraded to the 12v system.

This line had a great technical backbone. There were a number of automated and remote control features that allowed lights to shine in buildings, trains to uncouple, crossing-gate lights to flash, track switches to be thrown, and much more. Two or more controllers could be linked together to add more and more of these features to a home layout.

Model Train Scales

HOBBYISTS TALK ABOUT THEIR MODEL TRAINS IN TERMS OF THEIR SCALE. HO SCALE, FOR INSTANCE, IS 1/87 THE SIZE OF A REAL TRAIN CAR. FOR INSTANCE, IF A REAL TRAIN CAR IS 50 FEET LONG, DIVIDE BY 87, AND THE CAR SHOULD BE .5 FEET, OR 6 INCHES LONG.

G SCALE	1/22
O SCALE	1/48
HO SCALE	1/87
N SCALE	1/160
L GAUGE OR LEGO SCALE	ABOUT 1/38

- 9 VOLT (9V)
  The 9 volt system was introduced in 1991 and is still in production today. This line introduced stability and ease of use to the LEGO Train line. The 9v motors are a major leap forward because of the improved design and because the metal wheels on the specially designed train motors safely pull power directly from the metal rails. These wheels have minimal friction on the axle, rubber rims that help grip the rails, and a brilliant system of rubber bands that constantly push the metal wheels against the track for good contact.

This line also introduced the new track system—straight, curved, crossover, and switch tracks that include both the two rails and the ties in one-piece track modules.

In this book, we will be focusing entirely on the 9v line.

→ NOTE: *If you have 4.5v or 12v trains, you can make them 9v compatible simply by changing out the older wheels and motors for 9v versions. The dimensions of all three lines are basically the same.*

Okay, now's the time to get started! The rest of this book is divided into two sections. In the first part, "Fundamentals," we will cover the basics of the LEGO Train system. In the "Projects" section we will dive headfirst into building several train models. By the time you make it through this book, you will be well on your way to becoming a real live LEGO Train engineer!

CHAPTER 2

FUNDAMENTALS

The LEGO Train system is a simple system, and with a bit of background, you will be up and running in no time. Before you know it, you will be creating huge layouts and running great trains!

In the Fundamentals section we will look at:

- Your first LEGO Train set
- Locomotives and train cars
- LEGO Train track
- The speed regulator
- Running your trains

YOUR FIRST LEGO TRAIN SET

Getting started with LEGO Trains is quite easy. LEGO offers several train sets that come with all the necessary components to be up and running right out of the box. These sets typically come with a small oval track, a speed regulator, and a train motor. And, of course, they also come with a few train cars and accessories. Check your local toy store or LEGO Shop At Home (http://www.LEGOshop.com) for product availability.

If you want to build your own custom train layout, you have several options. To put together a starter set on your own, you will need:

- At least one locomotive with a motor
- At least one train car
- LEGO Train track
- A speed regulator (including AC power adaptor and track-connecting wire)

With this setup, you will be well on your way to your first layout.

TRAIN SETS

The LEGO Company offers several great starter train sets, complete with all the components you need to create your first LEGO Train layout. Everything you need to get started is in the box, so you will be up and running in no time.

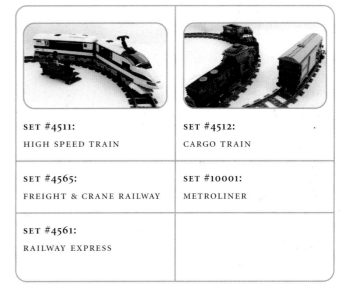

SET #4511:
HIGH SPEED TRAIN

SET #4512:
CARGO TRAIN

SET #4565:
FREIGHT & CRANE RAILWAY

SET #10001:
METROLINER

SET #4561:
RAILWAY EXPRESS

LOCOMOTIVES

Every train starts with the locomotive. Without it, a train doesn't have power, and without power a train can't go. Let's look at a few of the official LEGO locomotive sets. (Out of the box, these are great sets. Make sure to add a 9v motor unit to each one.)

Studs Not On Top (SNOT)

MOST OFFICIAL LEGO MODELS USE A STANDARD BUILDING PROCESS, STACKING BRICKS ON TOP OF EACH OTHER VERTICALLY. WE ARE USED TO SEEING THE STUDS (THOSE KNOBBY THINGS ON TOP OF EACH BRICK AND PLATE) POINTING UP.

MORE ADVANCED BUILDERS, AND SOME OFFICIAL SET DESIGNS, BUILD MODELS THAT USE A TECHNIQUE CALLED SNOT, OR STUDS NOT ON TOP. SNOT TECHNIQUES TAKE THE BRICKS AND PLATES AND TURN THEM IN ALL KINDS OF DIRECTIONS. THE STUDS CAN POINT UP, DOWN, OR SIDEWAYS.

SNOT ENABLES NOT ONLY THE CREATION OF SPECIALIZED SHAPES AND ANGLES, BUT ALSO VARIOUS NONSTANDARD DIMENSIONS. THESE DIMENSIONS CAN GET SMALLER THAN THE

TYPICAL ONE BRICK-ONE PLATE WIDTH. BOTH OF THESE ABILITIES ADD A WEALTH OF CONSTRUCTION TECHNIQUES AND DESIGNS.

FOR ADDITIONAL INFORMATION ON SNOT TECHNIQUES, PLEASE VISIT HTTP://WWW.BRICKSONTHEBRAIN.COM/TRAINS.

10020 SANTA FE SUPER CHIEF LOCOMOTIVE

The Super Chief locomotive LEGO model is based on the real Super Chief trains built in the United States in the 1950s and 1960s. These trains were painted with a vivid red and yellow color scheme called a "Warbonnet" scheme. Pulling the highly visible stainless steel silver passenger car, the Super Chief train was certainly something to see.

Not only does the LEGO version of this locomotive successfully recreate the Warbonnet color scheme, it also uses SNOT (studs not on top) techniques to create the beautiful rounded nose. This set also marked the first use of the light gray wheelsets. The Super Chief is a beautiful set and is a must build. (Figures 1 & 2)

MY OWN TRAIN STEAM ENGINE

The first of its kind, this official LEGO set allows you to cus-

tomize your own steam engine set. When you purchase one through LEGO Shop At Home (http://www.legoshop.com), you choose the style of locomotive, the color, and whether or not it includes a coal tender. Using the special Train Configurator application, you get to build the locomotive twice—once when you design it, and once when you assemble the model. You can even design a full custom train, with train cars and all. (Figure 3)

TRAIN CARS

A train without train cars is simply a locomotive. To put together a full train, you will need to add some train cars. There are a several ways you can obtain new train car sets Find out more at http://www.bricksonthebrain.com/trains.

10022 AND 10025 SANTA FE SUPER CHIEF CARS

Designed by LEGO fan James Mathis, these cars are based on the real Santa Fe Super Chief

1

3

2

train. Over the years, the real Super Chief ran many types of cars, and these sets allow builders to create the most common cars—five in all.

In set #10022, you can build one of three cars (observation car, dining car, or sleeping car). In set #10025, you can build one of two cars (mail car or baggage car). If you want to build all five cars at once, you will need three of set #10022 and two of set #10025.

When you put together a full train of five cars and two Super Chief locomotives (turned back to back), you'll have a very impressive train! (Figures 4 & 5)

ADDITIONAL TRAIN CARS

LEGO offers several more great train cars, like the Super Chief cars, as stand alone sets. They're listed to the right.

These cars are available from LEGO Shop At Home and in

SET #10013:

OPEN FREIGHT WAGON

These cars are used for carrying cargo, such as the included logs or other large cargo.

SET #10014:

CABOOSE

The caboose is one of the most recognized icons from railroading. This set is a must have for any cargo train!

SET #10015:

PASSENGER CAR

This passenger car is modeled after steam-engine era passenger cars. You could build a great passenger train with several of these cars.

SET #10016:

TANKER

A common site on today's railroads around the world, the tanker car can carry any kind of liquid. Oil, milk, and even maple syrup have all traveled in cars like this one.

SET #10017:

HOPPER

These cars are designed for carrying loose material like grain or gravel. Hoppers can dump their contents out of the bottom of the car, or like this model, out the sides.

SET #10002:

CLUB CAR

This car is a double-decker, with a sleeping area on the first deck and seats for viewing the land as you go by on the second deck. This car was designed as a wonderful complement to the Metroliner train.

selected retail stores, including the LEGO brand stores. To find a LEGO store near you, visit http://www.LEGO.com/legostores.

Once you have acquired your first LEGO Train set or put together a custom set, you have all the components you need to build your first train layout. Since we have already looked at train cars, what do you do next? Let's check out the track system.

LEGO TRAIN TRACK

The 9V LEGO Train track system is really quite ingenious. The track system is robust, easy to use, safe, and easily changed. It is made up of small sections of various shapes. Each section of track is a single molded piece with a thin metal sheet on top of the rails. These sections easily snap together with other section, which allows countless designs to be created, limited only by the amount of track you own and your imagination. (Figure 6)

The metal layer that wraps over the top of each rail safely conducts electricity, which is picked up by the metal wheels of the train motor and powers the train. This process is described in the "Tracks" chapter.

TYPES OF TRACK

LEGO track comes in four basic styles: straight, curve, switch, and cross. With these four styles you can create a great many track layouts.

STRAIGHT TRACK (SET #4515)

The most basic type of track is a straight. Just like the name implies, this is simply a straight length of track. As of this writing, there is only one type of straight track. Straights are 8 studs wide by 16 studs long. (Figure 7)

CURVE TRACK (SET #4520)

Another basic type of track is the curve. Compared to other types of electrical trains LEGO curved track has a fairly sharp radius, which makes for a pretty sharp turn. (Figure 8)

SWITCH TRACK (SET #4531)

Switch tracks, also known as *points*, can be added to the basic track layout to split one track into two. (These splits are often called *sidings* or *spur lines*; when connected on both ends, they are called passing lines). A switch is basically a length of straight track (2 standard straight tracks), with a curved track, or branch track, coming out of one side of the straight. There are two types of switches: one that curves to the left, and one that curves to the right. (Figure 9)

The switches are designed so that if you add one straight to the straight section, and one curve to the branch, both tracks will be in the same location and parallel.

Switches allow you to create all kinds of track layouts. For instance, you can have a main track (known as a *main line*) going around in a large circle,

---

Measurements of LEGO Bricks

LEGO ENTHUSIASTS REFER TO LEGO ELEMENTS BY STUDS — THOSE LITTLE KNOBS ON THE TOP OF A BRICK.

A 1×2 BRICK IS 1 STUD WIDE BY 2 STUDS LONG. A 2×2 BRICK IS 2 STUDS WIDE BY 2 STUDS LONG.

IF A BRICK IS TALLER THAN A NORMAL SINGLE BRICK, AN ADDITIONAL NUMBER IS ADDED TO THE DIMENSION NUMBERING. A 1×2×5 BRICK IS 1 STUD WIDE BY 2 STUDS LONG BY 5 BRICKS TALL.

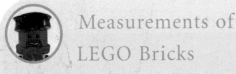
6

7

8

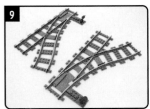
9

10

with a smaller length of track inside the loop (known as a *spur line, side rail, siding,* or *passing rail*). (Figure 10)

Electrical power can be supplied to either the main track or the spur line or both. This means that the track on the side rail can be dead, so you can have a train sitting on the side rail as another train is going around the main track. Or, you can add electrical power to both the side track and the main track at the same time. This would allow one train to move along the side track as another is moving along the main track. But be careful! When both trains are going, they could collide with each other. Usually you will only want to have one part of the

track powered at a time. With the flip of the switch, you can redirect trains from one track to another. (Figure 11)

You can switch tracks while the power is on, but if you do, you may create short circuits in the track, which will cause power to be lost in some part of the tracks. (Short circuits will be discussed in the "Tracks" chapter.)

→ **NOTE**: *These short circuits aren't dangerous and won't harm the track; they simply cause the track to loose power.*

CROSS TRACKS (SET #4519)
Cross tracks enable a layout to form a figure eight—a classic track pattern. (Figure 12)

LEGO Track

THE LEGO RAILS ARE MADE OF GERMAN SILVER. IT IS A METAL ALLOY CONTAINING NO TOXIC HEAVY METALS, AND IT PRESENTS NO DANGER TO PEOPLE ALLERGIC TO NICKEL. THE METAL COMPOSITION OF THE RAILS IS 64% COPPER, 24% ZINC, AND 12% NICKEL.

EVEN THOUGH THE RAILS CONDUCT ELECTRICITY, THIS TRACK SYSTEM IS VERY SAFE FOR CHILDREN, AS WELL AS PETS. STILL, LEGO TRAINS ARE BEST RUN INDOORS.

SPEED REGULATOR
The speed regulator allows you to control your trains. The speed regulator takes power from the wall outlet and channels it into the track. Using the yellow knob, you can control the direction of the train, as well as the speed.

The LEGO track system is designed to be used with only one Speed Regulator. Using the speed dial (the big yellow

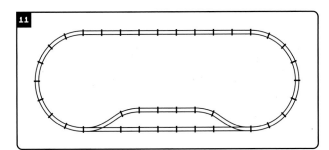

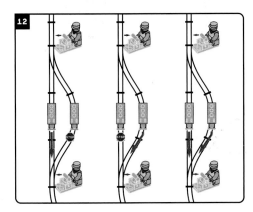

SPEED REGULATOR

TRANSFORMER
The transformer takes power from the wall outlet and feeds it to the speed regulator, which channels it into the track.

knob), you can control the direction and speed of your trains. If you put more than one motor on the track at one time, they will all be run at the same speed and direction.

Typically, you will only need one speed regulator for your track layout. However, if you create a very large track design, you may need to put two speed regulators on opposite ends to ensure that enough power is getting to the entire layout. If the track layout gets too big, the part of the track furthest away from the speed regulator will lose power. You will need to experiment with the setup to get it just right.

→ **NOTE**: *Even if you were to add an additional speed regulators, you wouldn't be able to control two (or more) trains on the same track separately. Both trains would be on or off at the same time. If you decide to use a second speed regulator, you should make sure to control both regulators in tandem. They should both be either on or off, just like using only one speed regulator.*

The transformer plugs into the wall and the power cord leading from it plugs into the side of the speed regulator. (The plug on the end of the transformer cord—a black cylindrical part—is a noise-suppression unit. It's there to avoid radio or television interference.)

→ **NOTE**: *There are two versions of the speed regulator—North American and European. Make sure that you are using the correct version. Each one has a different type of power cord.*

In order to power the track from the speed regulator, you need to attach the connecting wire to a section of track. Here's how to do it.

STEP 1

Attach the wire clips to both sides of the track so that the metal tabs contact the metal track. The wire clips click when they are properly locked in place.

STEP 2

Run track wire under the tracks. Each section of track has special notches cut to allow the track to sit flat on the ground.

STEP 3

Attach the connector plate from the track wire to the speed regulator.

STEP 4

Plug the transformer cord into the speed regulator. The yellow control knob on the speed regulator should be in the neutral position—o—or straight up and down.

STEP 5

Plug the transformer into the electrical outlet. The green light on the speed regulator should come on and glow brightly.

The LEGO Train Power System

ELECTRICITY FLOWS FROM THE WALL AT 120V AC (VOLTS OF ALTERNATING CURRENT) INTO THE TRANSFORMER. THE TRANSFORMER BREAKS THE VOLTAGE DOWN FROM 120V AC TO 12V AC, WHICH THEN FLOWS FROM THE TRANSFORMER INTO THE SPEED REGULATOR. THE SPEED REGULATOR DOES TWO THINGS: IT CONVERTS THE POWER FROM AC (ALTERNATING CURRENT) TO DC (DIRECT CURRENT), AND IT BREAKS THE 12V AC DOWN FURTHER TO THE RANGE OF 0V TO 9V. THE 9V OF ELECTRICITY TRAVELS FROM THE SPEED REGULATOR TO THE TRACK VIA THE CONNECTING LINK, THROUGH THE TRACK, AND UP THE METAL WHEELS TO THE TRAIN MOTOR, WHICH IS A 9V MOTOR.

SETTING UP YOUR FIRST LEGO TRAIN LAYOUT

Whether you have purchased an all-in-one train set like the #4511 or #4512, or you have acquired all the necessary components separately, getting set up is a piece of cake.

RUNNING YOUR TRAINS

Running your trains is very simple, and great fun! To the right are some steps for getting started.

The speed of your train depends on how much you turn the yellow control knob. The more you turn the knob away from 0 (straight up and down), the faster the train goes!

You can try to run as many cars on a track at once as you can fit. However, even with two motors, trains with more than about twenty cars start to have problems—the motors can't pull them very well.

The length of the train and the speed at which you can run it is highly dependent on the track layout. If the layout is a small oval, high speeds can send the train flying off the tracks. A very long train can be pulled much faster on a straightaway than on a curve. Try some different track designs and train lengths and pick what works well for you.

First, be sure that you have all the necessary components:

- One locomotive model or set
- One motor
- One train car model or set
- Enough track to form a circle
- Speed regulator and power transformer
- Connecting wire for the speed regulator

If your locomotive and train car designs aren't built yet, you should build them now.

Snap your track sections together to form a circle.

Connect the Speed Regulator, Transformer, and Connecting Wire as described above.

STEP 1
Place the locomotive on the tracks, making sure that all wheels make contact with the track.

STEP 2
Add the desired number of cars in the same fashion. Magnetic couplers connect cars and locomotives. Check that all car wheels are resting on the tracks and that the cars are coupled with the other train cars.

STEP 3
To operate the train, turn the yellow control knob clockwise; the train should move forward. If the train moves backward, turn the yellow knob in the opposite direction, change the track wire so that the connections touch the opposite tracks, or change the direction of the track wire on the speed regulator.

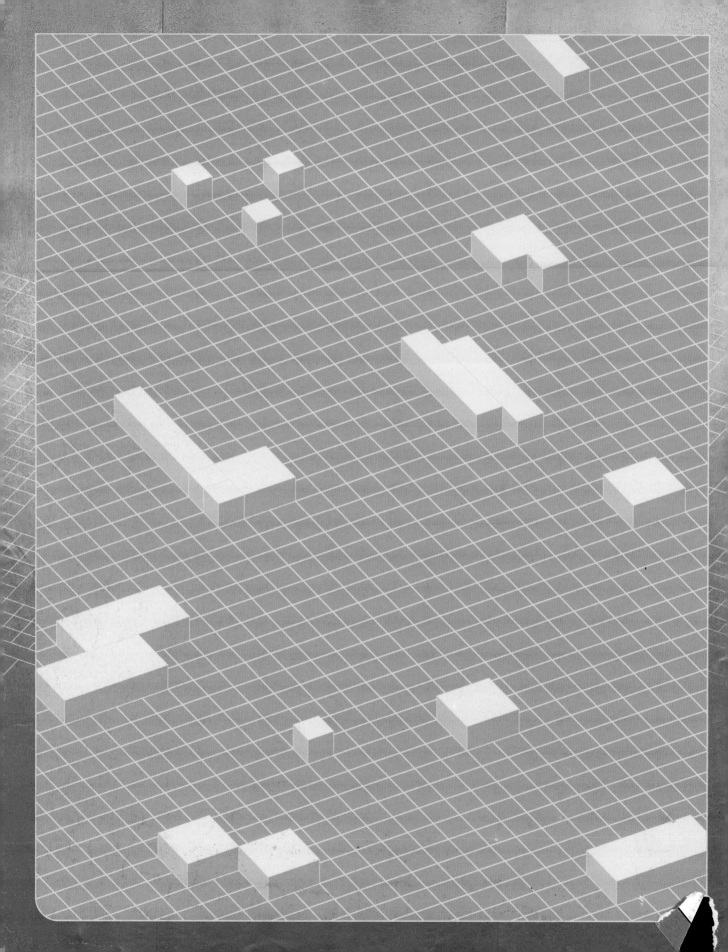

PART

2

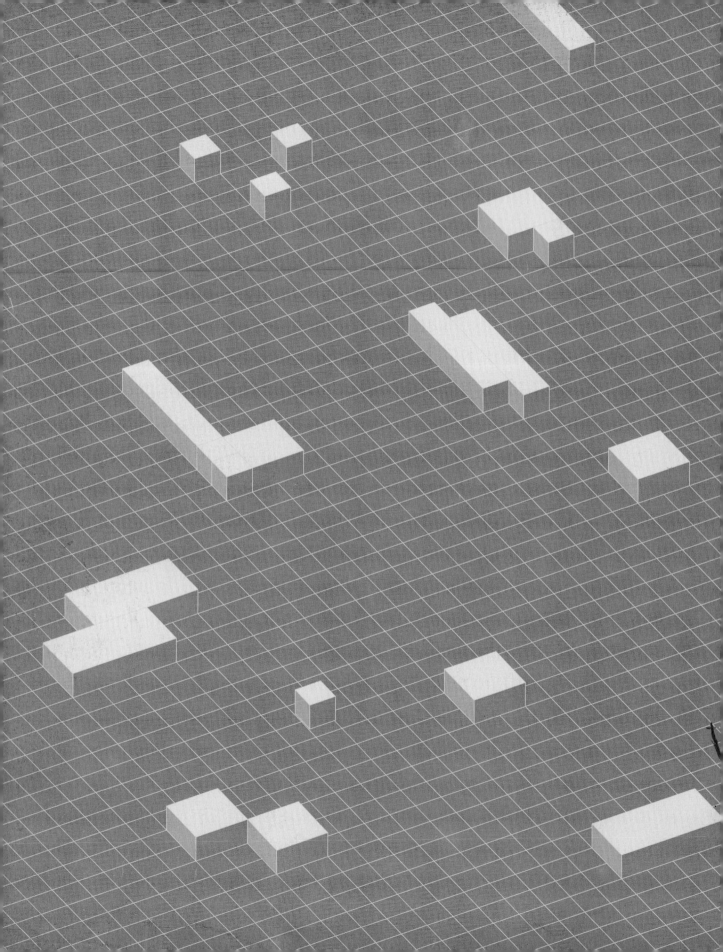

PROJECTS

By now, you have almost certainly built your first layout and run your LEGO Trains. If you're now thinking, "This is great, but what's next? How can I make the track layout bigger? How can I build my own cars based on my own designs?" you're on the road to becoming a LEGO Train engineer.

Let's move on to several projects that will walk you through creating specific train models. While you will be able to build the specific models shown by following the included instructions, these projects are meant to give you a basic understanding of train-building techniques so you can continue on to build your own creations at home.

Each project has full building instructions, and we will look at specific construction and detailing techniques showcased in each model. You'll be able to use these techniques in future models.

Our starter projects include:

- A modern North American-style locomotive
- A 1940s refrigerator car
- A modern intermodal container car

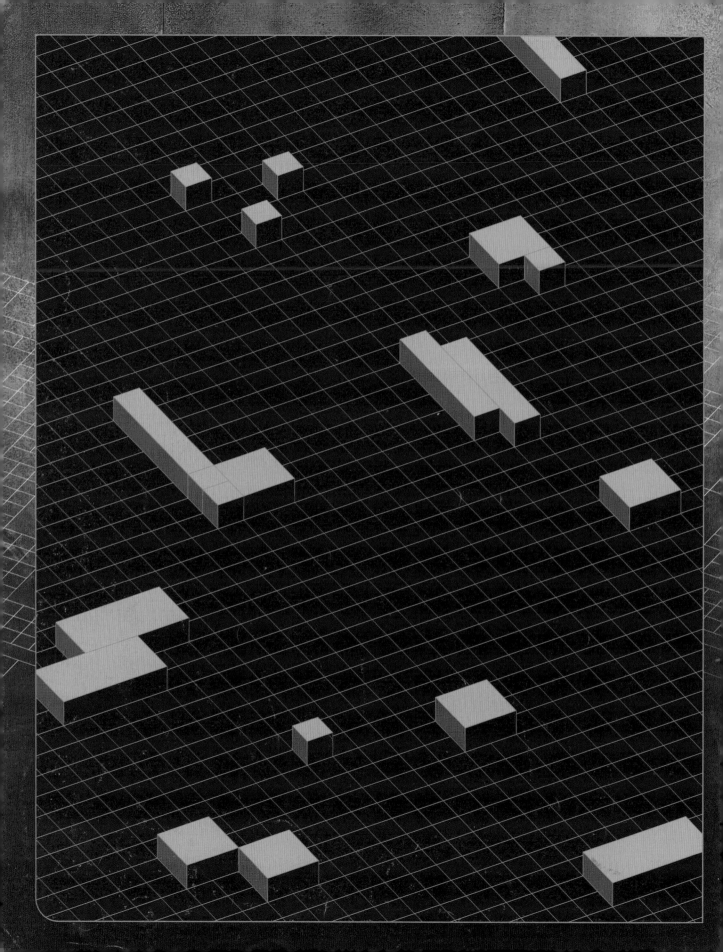

CHAPTER 3

TRAIN-BUILDING BASICS

Before we jump into building, let's look at several LEGO elements specifically designed for LEGO Trains. You will need to use most, if not all, of the parts listed here in order to build most LEGO Train designs.

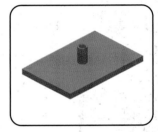

COUPLERS

The coupler on any real or model train attaches one car to another. LEGO Train couplers consist of two parts: a magnet that allows cars to hold on to one another, and the magnet holder.

BUFFERS

Buffers on real trains help to ensure that if two cars bump into each other, they don't damage one another. LEGO Train buffers attach to the train motor or wheelsets with a modified 2×2 smooth tile. The couplers are attached to the buffers.

WHEELS

The wheels allow train cars to run on the LEGO Train track. These wheels now come in two colors: all black, and gray with black wheels.

When a builder creates a design that combines two or more wheels, he has created a *wheelset*, or in railroading terms, a *truck* or *bogie*.

BOGIE PLATE

This 4×6 plate is smooth, and its top has a pin in the middle. The bogie plate is placed on top of a wheelset in order to attach that wheelset to the train car.

Because this plate is smooth on top, the wheelset can turn freely. The tapered edges allow the wheels to rotate when going over bumps in the track.

TRAIN BASE PLATES

These come in three types:

6×24 STUDS

6×28 STUDS

DROP BOTTOM

These base plates have three holes at both ends. The pin on the top of the bogie plate is used to attach wheelsets that use the bogie plate to the train baseplate. This baseplate also has two rectangular openings in the middle that allow a builder to run a LEGO electric wire from the train motor to the inside of a train model. This allows you to create train cars that use lights or motors.

DESIGN PROCESS

There is no one correct way to design LEGO trains; everyone designs differently. The most important thing is for you to find a design process that fits your skill level and interest in the LEGO Trains hobby. After all, if you aren't having fun, you probably won't be building LEGO Trains for long.

Personally, I enjoy creating LEGO Train models based on real-world designs. I like to make my trains as realistic as possible, so I rarely design my own cars (I recreate real cars). Because of this, the projects in this book will use building techniques and concepts that show how I've recreated several real-world designs in LEGO bricks.

→ NOTE: *If you are interested in designing your own cars from your imagination, you can certainly use the building techniques discussed in this book in your own designs. Why not design a train that explores other themes, like a space train, or an underwater submarine train? Let your imagination run wild!*

CHOOSING A DESIGN

The first step in any design process is to figure out what to build. Since trains have been around for more than a hundred years, there are lots of great designs to borrow from. To find an interesting design, you might surf the Internet, browse train books at your local library, or visit local train museums. And be sure to look for designs from around the world—there are many design differences between real-world trains in North American and Europe, for instance.

Before you begin recreating a real design, collect images of your chosen train car or locomotive (sometimes called a *loco* for short) that show as many angles as possible. Front, right side, left side, and ¾ view are a minimum. The more angles you can get, the easier it will be to visualize the overall shape of the locomotive and to create an accurate design.

In addition to these basic overall photos, try to find some pictures or technical drawings that show the locomotive or train car up close. The more you know of the real details, the better you will be able to choose just the right ones to make your model look highly realistic.

CHAPTER 4

GP-38 LOCOMOTIVE

For our first project, we'll start with the head of the train: the loco-motive. There are all kinds of real locomotives to choose from. Everything from old steam engines to modern diesel-electric locos to trolleys to mountain railways, just to name a few.

We'll create a LEGO version of the GP-38, a popular modern North American diesel-electric locomotive. (Figure 1)

COLOR SCHEME

When choosing the color scheme for your design, you can choose any color combi-nation that is within the LEGO color palette. You can either pick your own colors or match the scheme of a real-world design. The nice thing is that any color scheme you come up with has probably been used on some railroad at some point in time.

→ NOTE: *Don't forget to con-sider your parts selection when choosing a color scheme. If you choose to make an orange loco, but you don't have any orange windows or bricks, you might have problems.*

For our first locomotive, we'll use the Union Pacific color scheme shown here. (Figure 2)

Now let's get to work!

Railroad Names

OVER THE LAST CENTURY, THERE HAVE BEEN A GREAT MANY RAILROADS. EACH HAD A CUSTOM NAME, LOGO, AND COLOR SCHEME. RAILROADERS OFTEN REFER TO THE RAILROAD'S NAME AS ITS **ROADNAME**, AND ITS COLOR SCHEME AS **LIVERY**.

AS COMPANIES WERE BOUGHT AND SOLD, ROADNAMES, AS WELL AS COLOR SCHEMES AND LOGOS, WERE CHANGED AND MODIFIED. RAILROADERS HAVE JOKED FOR SOME TIME THAT IF YOU CAN DREAM UP A COLOR SCHEME, YOU CAN PROBABLY FIND A LOCO- MOTIVE OR A TRAIN CAR THAT ONCE WORE THAT COLOR SCHEME.

REFERENCE MATERIALS

The next step is to find some photos of a real GP-38 loco- motive. Since we are simply trying to get a solid under- standing of the overall design, it doesn't matter whether these photos are of the right color scheme and roadname. They simply need to be of the right locomotive—in this case a GP-38. Some sample photos are shown below.

Once you have found some pic- tures, make photocopies of them, or print them from your computer, and have them handy so you can easily refer to them during the design process.

OVERALL DIMENSIONS AND PROPORTIONS

With photos in hand, it's time to start laying the groundwork for the locomotive. But first we need to answer some basic questions:

- Will the loco be 6 studs wide or 8 studs wide?

- Will the loco use a standard train base plate? If so, will it be 24 studs long or 28 studs long?

- Will it be built to be basically the same size as the official LEGO Trains?

As you build more and more LEGO Trains and train layouts, this list of initial questions will continue to grow. Do you have enough parts to build a full train, rather than just one or two cars? Is your car too long to easily go around curves?

For the GP-38, I decided to use the LEGO Train base plate, rather than creating my own locomotive base plate out of multiple LEGO plates. In order to get the design to look right, I wanted the loco as long as pos- sible to keep the right proportions. Even when using the longer 6×28 train base plate, it still seemed too short.

To remedy this problem, I added endcaps, or extensions that extend each end of the locomo- tive by three studs on each end—six studs in total. This doesn't sound like much, but those extra six studs made the loco almost 20 percent longer. (Figure 3)

→ **NOTE**: *Be careful with this endcap technique. The endcaps should look like they are part of the train base plate. If you go much more than three studs past the train baseplate, the plates start to droop, which makes it obvious that it is an add-on endcap.*

Once I decided on the overall length, it was time to start plan- ning the rest of the design.

SETTING THE PROPORTIONS

Before I started to build this model, I had to figure out the proportions of the loco. This helped me understand how much of the design should be allotted to the cab, how much to the hood, and so on. To start the task of proportioning, I first broke down each section of the real-world locomotive as shown here. (Figure 4)

Most of these types of locomo- tives will break down into some easy-to-define sections. As you can see in the previous image, the GP-38 locomotive broke down into four sections (from left to right):

- Rear deck and rear section of the loco body
- Main section of loco body
- Cab section
- Front decking and train nose

Once I had these sections, I started placing outline bricks on the train base plate (with endcaps in place) to mark where each section should start and stop. Don't worry too much about being perfect at this stage. You will most likely have to make changes later in the design process. The key here is to get a good feel for how the size of each section relates to the other sections.

Early on in my design process, I realized that the cab area was going to be tight. I really wanted to be able to remove the roof to add or remove the LEGO Minifig engineer (a *Mini-figure* is one of those little LEGO people, often called a *minifig*). This meant that, at a minimum, the cab had to be able to fit a minifig chair and have room for the minifig arms. (Figure 5)

Before I knew it, I had a starting point for the design.

DESIGNING COMPONENTS

Early on in your designs, you will notice that one or more design elements stand out from the others. It's important to find these elements, because the rest of the design process hinges on getting them nailed down early on. In this case, the cab was obviously the first thing that I needed to focus on, so I built a rough version of it, simply to determine the appropriate size for the minifig.

The next major features to build were the coolers on the left side of the loco. Fortunately, in my design process, I had found several pictures that showed these coolers. (As mentioned earlier, it is important to find pictures of the real-world version from all angles.)

Using the half-stud trick, I offset the cooler so that it stuck out past the train body by half the width of a 1-stud-wide brick. The half width made the cooler look much more realistic. Additionally, this technique allowed me to keep the train body 4 studs wide — anything less would have looked quite odd.

6 vs. 8 Studs Wide

LEGO TRAINS CAN BE BUILT TO BE ANY SIZE YOU WANT, THOUGH ALL OFFICIAL LEGO TRAINS ARE BUILT TO BE 6 STUDS WIDE. (LEGO MODELS ARE "MEASURED" BY THE NUMBER OF STUDS.)

IN RECENT YEARS, MANY PEOPLE HAVE STARTED TO BUILD THEIR TRAINS 8 STUDS WIDE, AND SOME DESIGNS ARE EVEN IN 7 WIDE. A FEW LEGO TRAIN FANS HAVE EVEN GONE AS BIG AS 14 WIDE!

THE LEGO TRAINS RUNNING THROUGH MINILAND AT ALL FOUR LEGOLAND PARKS (WWW.LEGOLAND.COM) ARE BUILT 18 STUDS WIDE. BECAUSE THEY RUN OUTSIDE ON SPECIAL TRACKS, THEY USE WHEELS AND MOTORS THAT ARE CUSTOM-MADE FOR THE PARKS. OTHERWISE, THE TRAINS ARE ALL BUILT OUT OF LOTS AND LOTS OF LEGO BRICKS.

Two other components are important for the overall design layout: the nose and the rear train body. Since both of these components need to look somewhat rounded, I knew I would need to use SNOT techniques.

Without worrying too much about the actual design, I built a version of both of these components to get a sense of overall size. I test-fit these in the brick outlines to see how I was doing.

After some adjustments to the brick outline, I was confident I had the right brick outline.

STARTING TO BUILD

Once you have established the basic layout with the outline bricks, and you have created a "first draft" of the major design components, it's time to start building the main loco body and to develop the real cab.

The Half-Stud Trick

ONE OF THE BEST AND MOST-USED BUILDING TECHNIQUES IS THE HALF-STUD TRICK. TYPICALLY WHEN BUILDING LEGO MODELS, BRICKS AND PLATES CAN ONLY BE OFFSET BY A FEW BRICK WIDTHS.

HOWEVER, BY USING THE 1X2 PLATE WITH ONE STUD ELEMENT, YOU CAN MOVE BRICKS AND PLATES BY ONLY HALF A STUD. IN THE GP-38 MODEL, THE COOLER, FOR INSTANCE, NEEDED TO POP OUT FROM THE SIDE OF THE LOCOMOTIVE, BUT NOT EXTEND ALL THE WAY TO THE SIDE OF THE LOCOMOTIVE. AS SHOWN HERE, THE HALF STUD TRICK SAVES THE DAY.

AS YOU BUILD MORE AND MORE LEGO MODELS, YOU WILL FIND THAT THIS BUILDING TECHNIQUE IS VERY USEFUL.

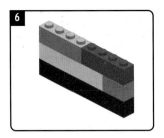

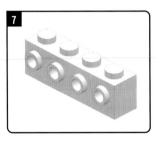

I like to keep the initial build of the entire model fairly simple. I don't worry too much about details, or even about including all of the design elements. The purpose of the first build is simply to make sure that all the proportions work well. (In fact, my first versions often are built in mostly light gray, which helps me to pay attention to the overall design, rather than to the color scheme. Light gray is a great color for this purpose because it is neutral and fairly plentiful.)

Once you have the basic shape down, it's time to start building a second, semi-final build. I say *semi-final*, because you will probably build and rebuild several times. The fact that you can do this is what makes LEGO such a great material to build with.

→ **NOTE**: *As you start to build a semi-final version, make sure to "cross your lines." This phrase, coined by fellow LEGO Train buff, Steve Barile, several years ago simply means that you*

should have as many seams between bricks (lines) overlapping each other as possible. This will substantially increase the model's stability. (Figure 6)

At this point, you will also need to determine how you are going to use SNOT techniques to attach the nose and rear body components. For both components, I used 1×4 bricks with studs on top and on one side. (Figure 7)

The placement of this brick is extremely important. If you place it too high in the model, the component you are trying to attach will sit too high. If you place the brick too low, you won't be able to properly attach the component. You will need to play with the adjustments for this brick; add and subtract plates and change its height to find the right height setting.

DETAILING THE LOCOMOTIVE BODY

Since you can't include every detail from a real-world locomotive in your LEGO Train model, you have to practice selective compression. This means that you must choose the most important details to be included in your design, effectively compressing or reducing the total number of details while still producing the desired, realistic effect.

Another aspect of selective compression is parts selection. When you focus on only the most important details, you have to make sure you can actually obtain the needed LEGO parts. If not, then you need to do some more compression.

When building the Union Pacific GP-38, I used several techniques to make the train body and cab exterior really pop. At the end of this chapter you will find full building

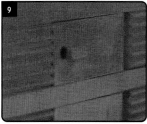

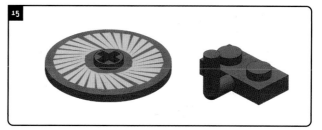

instructions for this model. I've highlighted the following techniques to show what can be done with some basic construction methods.

ACCESS DOORS

The real GP-38 has several access doors on each side. These doors allow train crews to perform repairs on the engine when needed. (Figure 8)

By using several LEGO car-door parts in the same color as the train body, I was able to recreate the effect of having many engine-access doors. The combination of the door handle and the curved end of the door makes for a great realistic look.

ADDITIONAL SIDEWALL TEXTURING

The access doors add a certain amount of texture to the sides of the locomotive model, but the model could use some more.

Note in the building instructions that the car doors are set two studs apart. This leaves room to insert one of my favorite texture bricks — the 1×2 corrugated. These bricks have a striped texture on both sides — both vertical and horizontal. (Figure 9)

Place the corrugated bricks between the doors, with the striping turned side to side. This texture looks nothing like the real-world version, but no matter. The simple fact that there is some type of texture provides the sense of realism.

The top side of the GP-38 has several vents and cooling grilles. To replicate these details, you can again use the corrugated bricks, but this time use the vertical striping to produce a different feel. (Figure 10)

UNION PACIFIC DECALS

To match the lettering on the real-world GP-38, I used decals

to recreate the Union Pacific logo text. (For more information on how to use decals, see the sidebar on the next page.)

To make sure that I had a flat surface to place the decal on, I designed the train body with a standard 1×12 brick on each side. This ensures that the decals will be applied to the correct area. (Figure 11)

CAB DECORATION

Because the sides of the cab seemed too flat, I added 1×2 tiles under the windows. The tiles are held in place by 1×1 headlight bricks. These tiles can be left blank (simply to add texture), or you can add decals to make the effect even more realistic. (Figures 12 & 13)

FANS

When designing the cooling fans on top of the locomotive, I used a technique that I borrowed from the Santa Fe Super Chief locomotive set (set #10020).

This brings up an important point: when designing LEGO models, it's important to develop your own techniques, but its equally important to learn from other great designers.

For this technique, simply add three of the 1×2 plate with arm parts to the top of the locomotive. Then slip three Technic disc parts over the top of the vertical arm. (Figures 14 & 15)

ROOF DETAILS

By adding some printed tiles and 1×2 grille tiles, you can really enhance the realism of the roof. I've also added a small lever to represent a radio antenna. (Figure 16 on the next page)

REMOVABLE CAB ROOF

For this design, I have given the cab a removable roof, which allows access to the cab to view details or to move a minifig in or out.

As you can see here, the roof is held in place by six studs (three on each of the front corners). This makes the roof somewhat difficult to remove, but sometimes you have to pick the lesser of two design evils. (Figure 17)

RAILING

I added simple railing with TECHNIC tubing and the arms from the Life on Mars aliens. (Figure 18)

TRUCKS AND GAS TANKS

The locomotive is almost done, except for some undercarriage details and the trucks. Let's finish it off.

TRUCKS

The wheelsets on a train are called *trucks*, and they not only hold the wheels of the train,

allowing the loco to move along the rails, but they also hold the couplers that allow the loco to pull train cars. After several design versions, I decided to use the standard train buffer and coupler.

The biggest design challenge with the trucks came when adding the steps. The front and rear of a real GP-38 have fixed steps to allow engineers to climb onto the locomotive. If our LEGO model had fixed steps, it would have caused all kinds of problems. Fixed stairs would have required the coupler to be attached not to the trucks but to the locomotive itself. When the loco went around curves, the coupler would have swung out too far

and pulled the coupler magnets apart.

Instead, I designed the trucks to include two of the three steps. The remaining step was added to the front and rear ends of the locomotive body. (Figure 19)

GAS TANK

Because locomotives have huge engines and burn a lot of fuel as they pull their long trains, they need huge gas tanks. The gas tank is underneath the locomotive body, between the front and rear trucks.

→ NOTE: *Make sure that this component doesn't interfere with the track. You don't want your locomotive to snag the track and derail.*

Since there is limited space in which to work, the details have to be subtle. Key design elements to replicate include a rounded design, like the real-life version, and the gas cap. This minor detail adds a great deal of realism.

When you build the gas tank, the building instructions will walk you through some easy SNOT techniques that

make it easy to mount the gas tanks under the locomotive. (Figure 20)

FINAL THOUGHTS

Soon you will have your first semi-final version of your locomotive. If you are anything like me, you will never feel like you are done with the design, and you will continue to build and rebuild. In fact, the locomotive that was the subject of this project has undergone at least seven major revisions. Keep building and tweaking your designs. As you tweak even small details, you will get ideas for both major revisions and minor details.

And don't forget to run the locomotive on a track layout. There is nothing like seeing your model in action to give you all kinds of ideas and inspiration. Also, you want to ensure that your designs can actually run smoothly on the tracks.

INTERVIEW WITH JAMES MATHIS ON BUILDING LEGO LOCOMOTIVES

James Mathis is perhaps best known in the LEGO fan community for being the second LEGO fan to be selected to

Decals

DECALS ARE A GREAT WAY TO ADD GRAPHICS TO YOUR TRAIN MODELS. MODEL RAILROADERS HAVE BEEN USING DECALS FOR DECADES TO ADD RAILROAD NAMES, TRAIN CAR NUMBERS, AND EVEN GRAFFITI.

FOR MORE INFORMATION ON APPLYING DECALS, CHECK OUT THE HTTP://WWW.BRICKSONTHEBRAIN.COM/TRAINS WEB SITE.

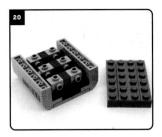

cooperate in the LEGO "My Own Creation" series. He created the original Santa Fe Super Chief train car designs for LEGO sets #10022 and #10025.

James frequently collaborates with individuals on train-model building projects through online discussions and sharing. These shared projects inspire him to find new solutions to specific design constructions as well as to learn new techniques from the work of others. Fan-created CAD programs have accelerated the realization and proliferation of design ideas as they are shared electronically across continents and oceans. James has taken advantage of this new virtual construction medium to create designs that would otherwise be very difficult, if not impossible, were he limited to only his personal brick collection.

• • •

Jake: James, you build some excellent locomotives. Tell us about your basic design process?

James: For models resembling real-life trains, I begin by browsing for pictures of trains and rolling stock. I look for pictures on the Internet, in books, and in magazines. Occasionally, I get to see real-life trains in person and will take pictures.

Sometimes, I will work on a fanciful model, or maybe even a fanciful train. That idea is usually stimulated by focusing on using a very specific LEGO element—say a certain wind-screen style. The train design then flows outward from that specific element. Many times a model of a specific real-life train is also initiated by seeing how a specific LEGO element resembles a key design form of the real-life train.

Once I have my model inspiration and initial starting point, the design process starts with MLcad, a computer-based LEGO CAD drawing and construction program. Any specific model usually starts with a base plate for a ground and dimensional point of reference. I then identify critical design form points, such as windscreen, side-window location, roof height, handlebars, railing, and nose end-point. The rest of the construction becomes filler to connect these critical design points.

Color Schemes

FOR THIS PROJECT, WE FOCUSED ON ONE COLOR SCHEME, BUT IT IS GREAT FUN TO CREATE DIFFERENT COLOR SCHEMES USING THE SAME BASIC DESIGN.

EACH TIME YOU CREATE A NEW COLOR SCHEME, YOU WILL NEED TO TWEAK THE DESIGN TO MAKE IT WORK. SOMETIMES THESE TWEAKS ARE VERY SMALL, BUT THEY CAN BE QUITE LARGE.

FOR EXAMPLE, CREATING A SANTA FE FREIGHT LOCOMOTIVE WITH THE WARBONNET DESIGN REQUIRED A MAJOR REWORKING OF THE CAB AND TRAIN BODY AREAS. HOWEVER, YOU CAN SEE THAT MUCH OF THE REST OF THE MASTER DESIGN REMAINS.

THIS GREEN BURLINGTON NORTHERN COLOR SCHEME IS AN EARLIER DESIGN (NOTICE THE OPENING ENGINE DOORS NOT FOUND IN LATER DESIGNS).

NOTE: SINCE THE 1X2X2 WINDOWS AREN'T CURRENTLY PRODUCED IN GREEN, I HAD TO SUBSTITUTE WHITE WINDOWS INSTEAD. IN THIS INSTANCE, THE SUBSTITUTION WORKS WITH THE OVERALL DESIGN. FOR MORE INFO ON FINDING PARTS, REFER TO APPENDIX B.

One great aspect of initially designing with a CAD program is that I can easily explore many alternate constructions—disassembly of the model and rearrangement of the pieces is very easy. I can also manipulate, flip, turn, and nudge elements into a variety of orientations. This allows me to find very unique ways of interlocking elements on their side or upside down.

Once I think I've got a good and potentially buildable version of the model, it's then time to do a "real brick build" test! Sometimes I'll just build a portion of the model if there seems to be a section that is of questionable integrity. Otherwise, I print out a parts list, gather the necessary parts, and begin a real brick build.

For a good final model, I sometimes print out the instruction steps. In this way, I can enjoy a "set build." I've gathered all the required pieces and I've got the instructions. It's almost like building an official LEGO set.

Jake: Great info! So what do you find to be the most difficult thing to build?

James: The sleek nose of a high-speed passenger train is very challenging. These real-life trains have some very complex slopes and curving geometries. Approximating these complex curves in the space six studs wide for a "standard" LEGO train can be a tough build using standard slopes, plates, and bricks. However, the assortment of complex curve elements from LEGO is increasing, and the possible constructions evolve along with new elements. The complex high-speed train nose is a wonderful puzzle to challenge my creativity.

Jake: What is your favorite creation you have built so far?

James: I'm very pleased with my active-tilting passenger train modeled after the British Rail Advanced Passenger Train (APT). Imitating the real-life train, the LEGO train cars tilt inward through curves. Tilting

of the cars through curves in real-life allowed for increased train speeds without disturbing a passenger's level of comfort.

I'm most proud of my participation in the creation of the official LEGO Trains sets #10022 and #10025 — companion passenger cars for the Santa Fe Super Chief train, which complement locomotive #10020.

Jake: What else would you tell a new LEGO Train fan just getting started?

James: Start simple and learn along the way. Build official sets and see how the master builders do it. That's all I did. Lots and lots of building for three decades.

One of the beautiful aspects of building anything with LEGO elements is that your models of today will become the basis for your models of tomorrow: reusing the bricks, rebuilding, and improving a design. Building with LEGO toys can be as challenging and as rewarding as you like. Just have fun.

→ **NOTE**: *For pictures of James' creations, check out www. brickshelf.com/cgi-bin/gallery. cgi?m=jamathis. For more information on fan created LEGO CAD software, check out www. ldraw.org.*

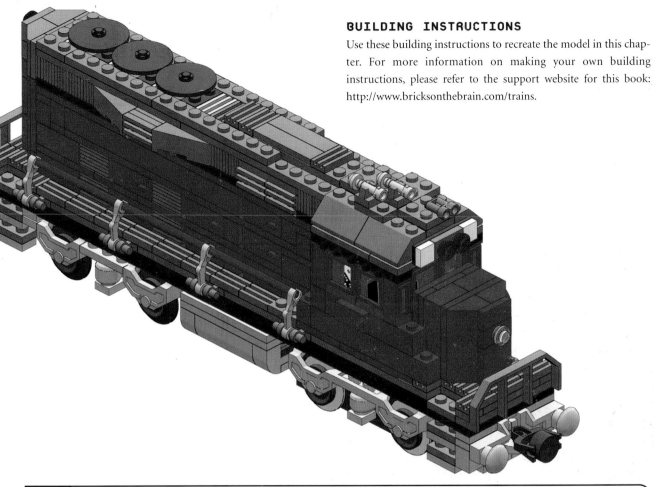

BUILDING INSTRUCTIONS

Use these building instructions to recreate the model in this chapter. For more information on making your own building instructions, please refer to the support website for this book: http://www.bricksonthebrain.com/trains.

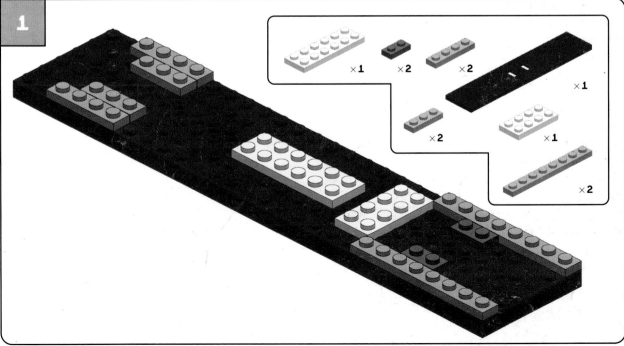

2

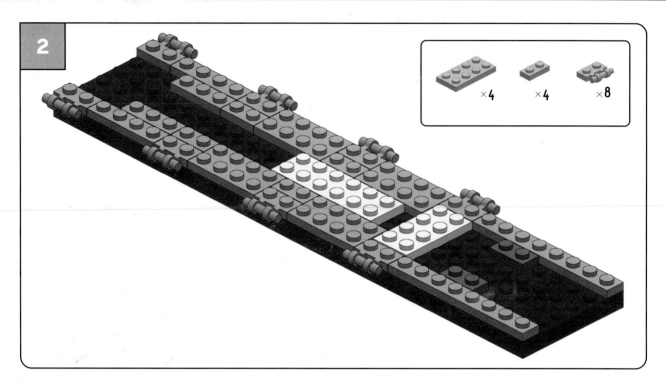

×4   ×4   ×8

3

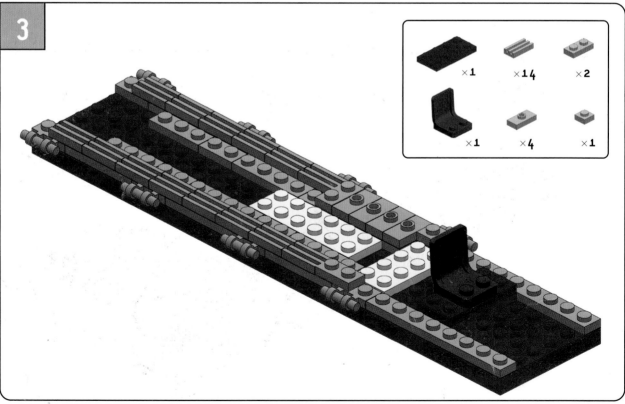

×1   ×14   ×2

×1   ×4   ×1

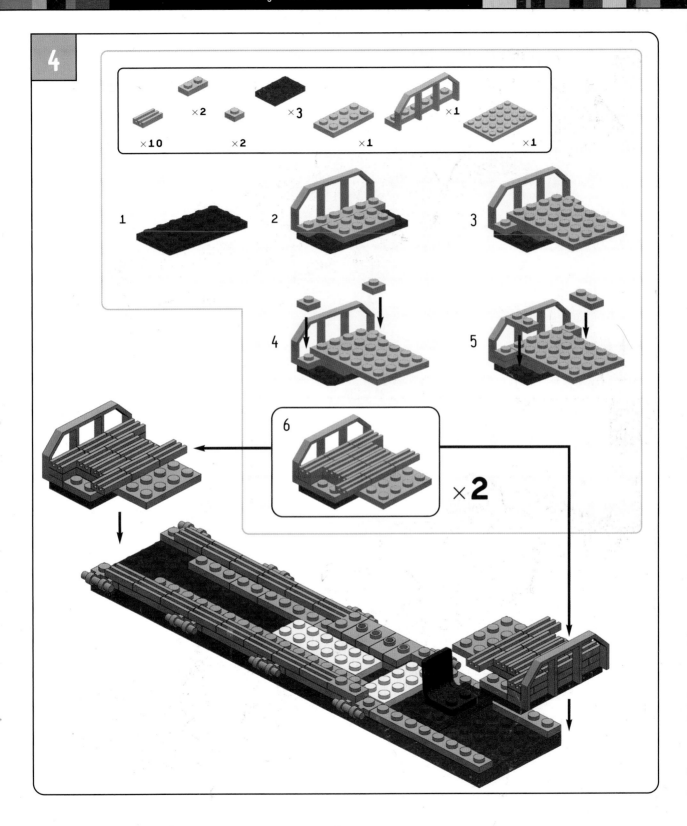

5

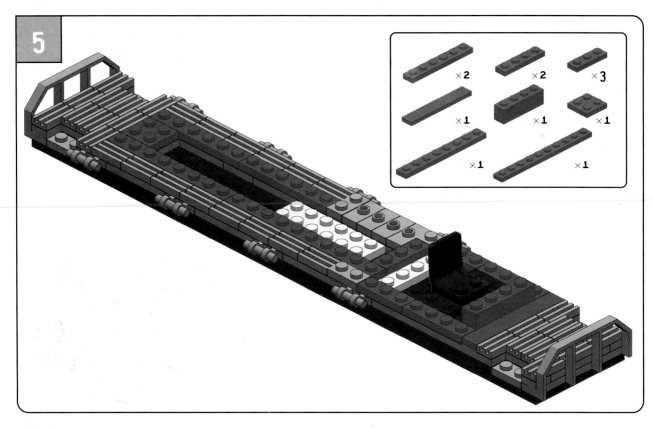

6

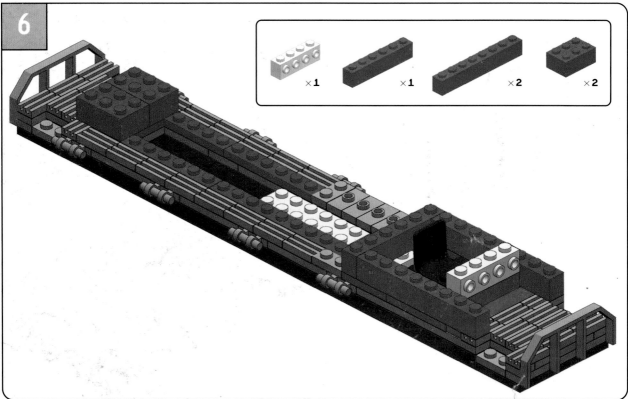

7

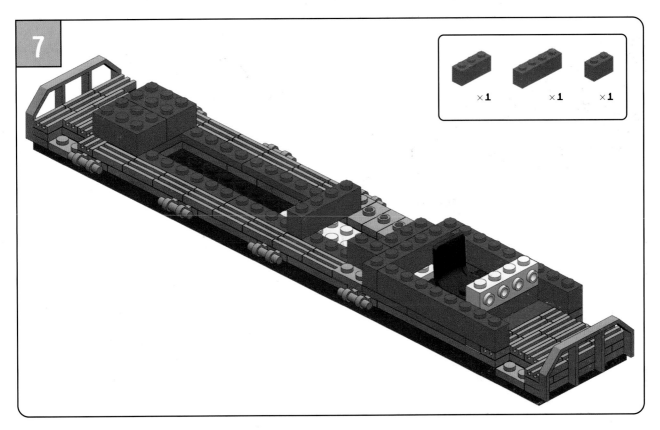

×1   ×1   ×1

8

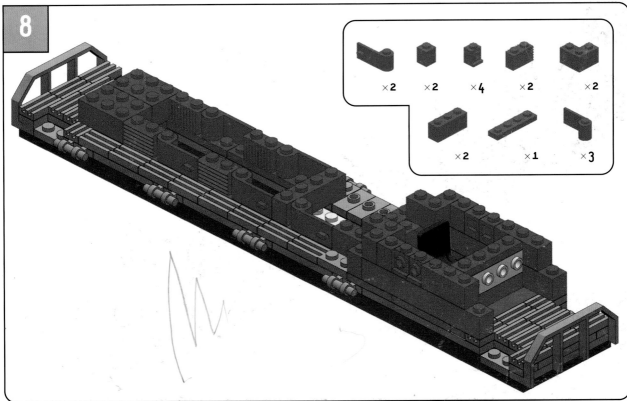

×2   ×2   ×4   ×2   ×2

×2   ×1   ×3

9

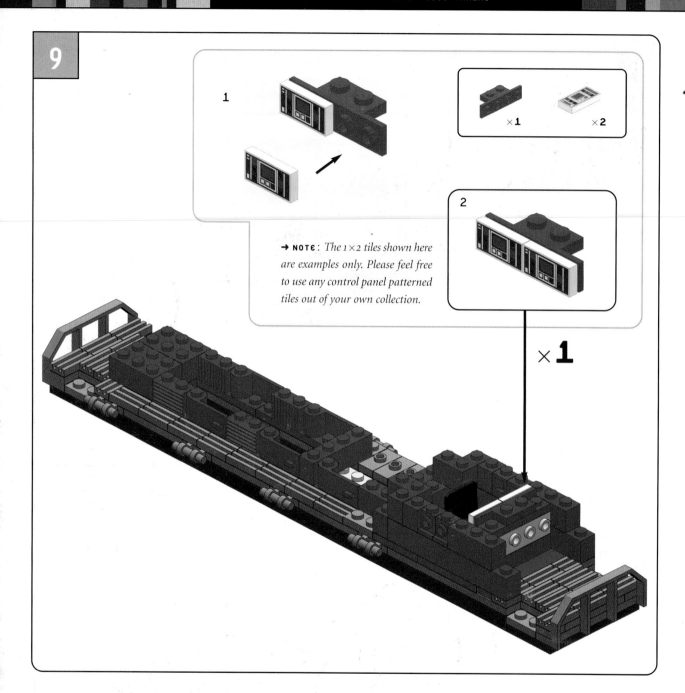

1

×1   ×2

2

→ **NOTE**: *The 1×2 tiles shown here are examples only. Please feel free to use any control panel patterned tiles out of your own collection.*

×**1**

10

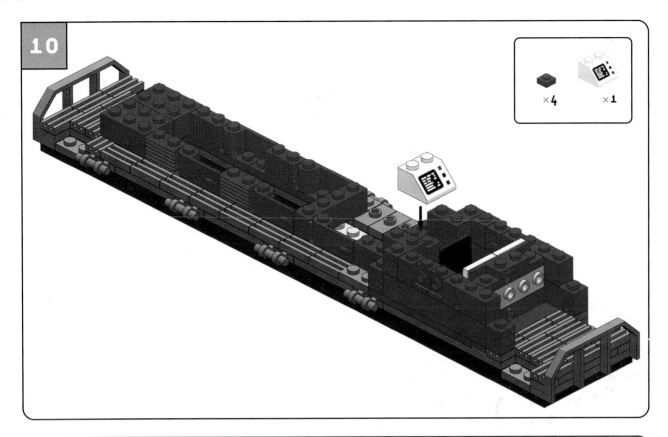

×4 ×1

11

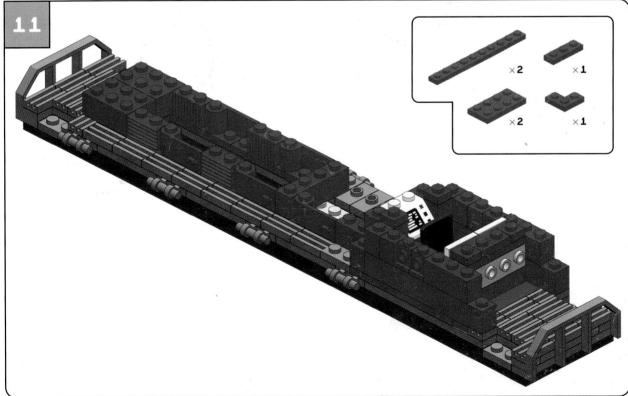

×2 ×1
×2 ×1

12

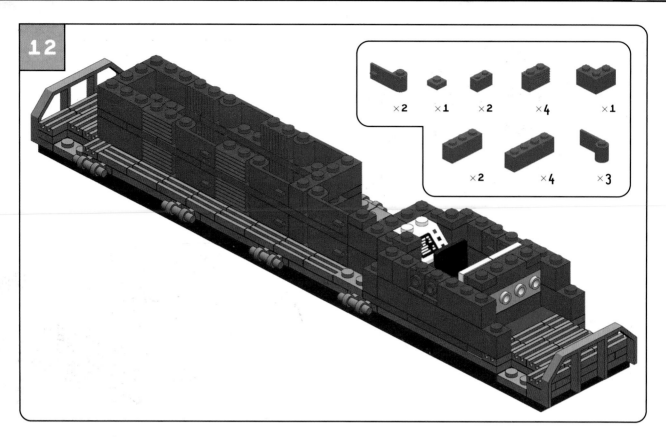

$\times 2$ $\times 1$ $\times 2$ $\times 4$ $\times 1$

$\times 2$ $\times 4$ $\times 3$

13

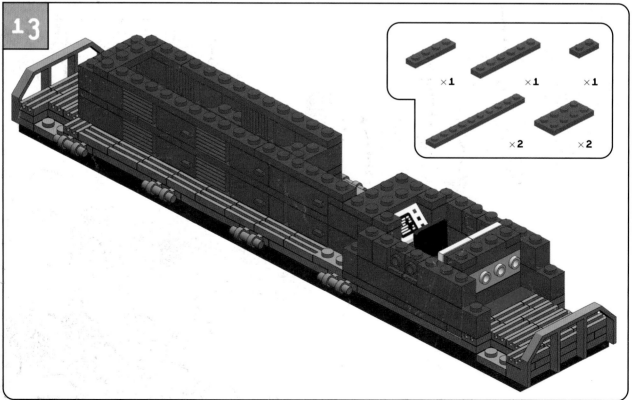

$\times 1$ $\times 1$ $\times 1$

$\times 2$ $\times 2$

14

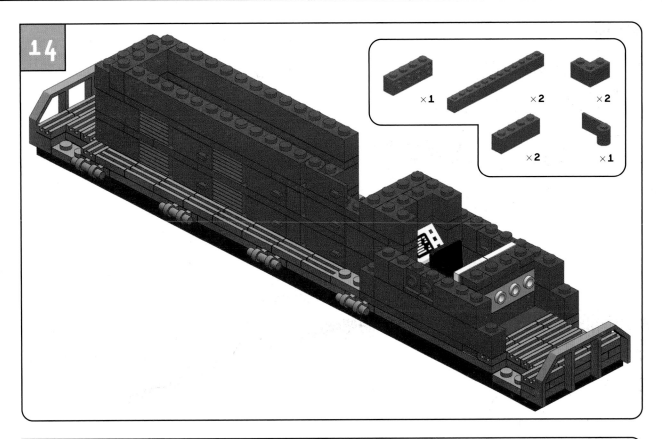

15

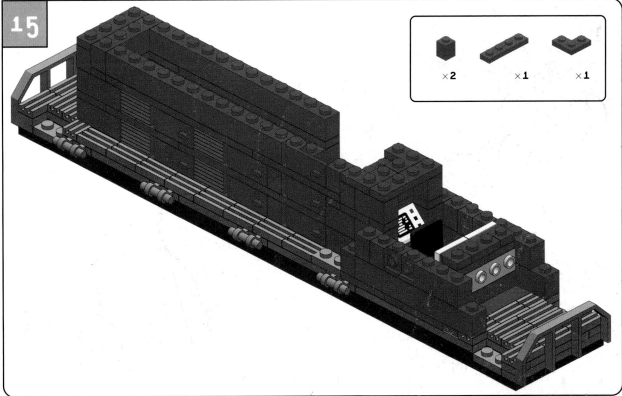

16

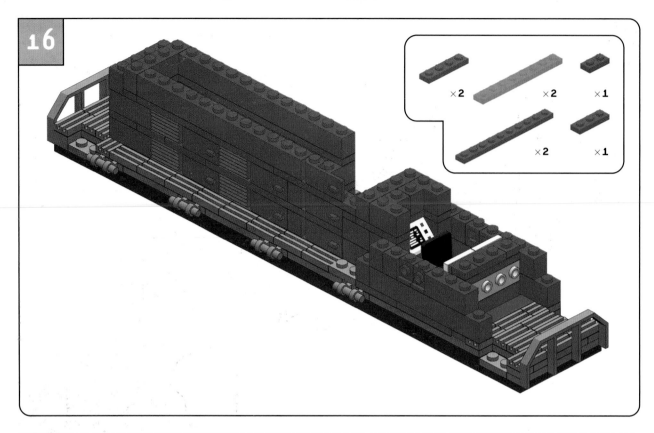

×2   ×2   ×1

×2   ×1

17

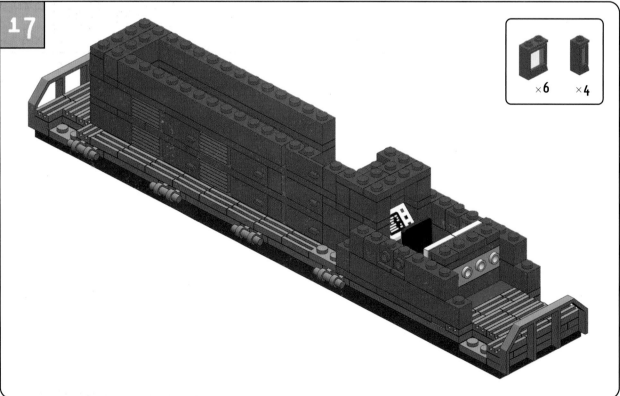

×6   ×4

18

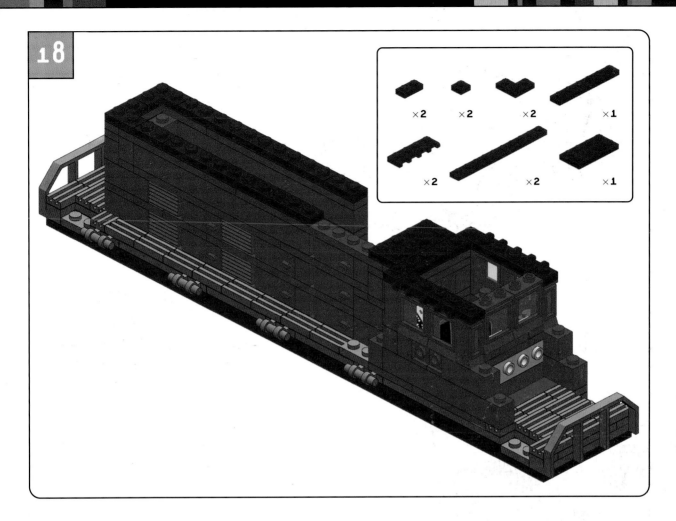

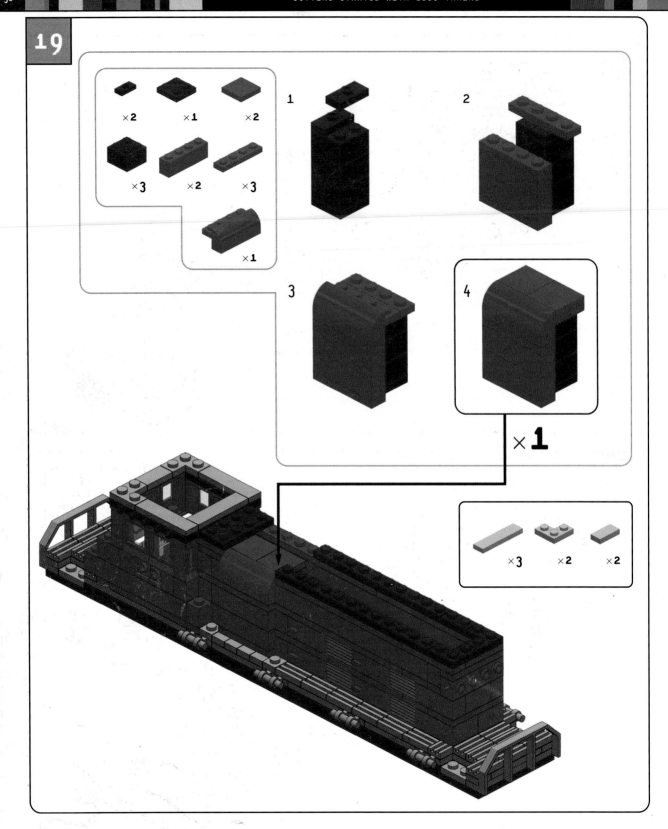

20

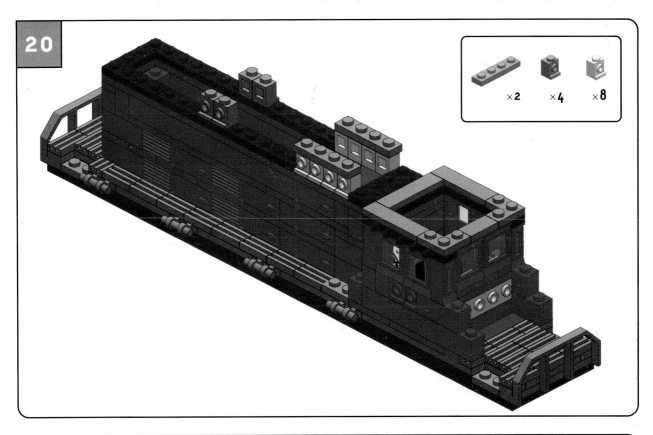

×2 ×4 ×8

21

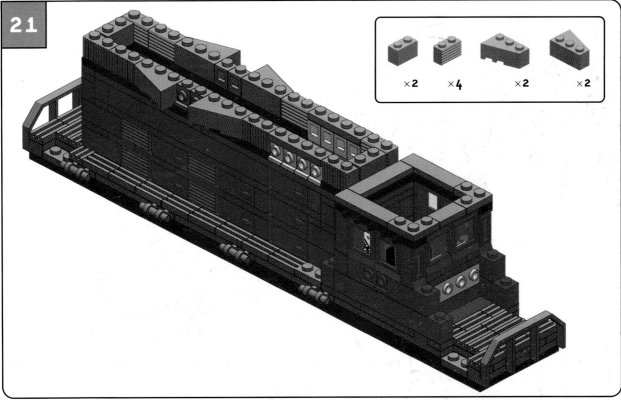

×2 ×4 ×2 ×2

22

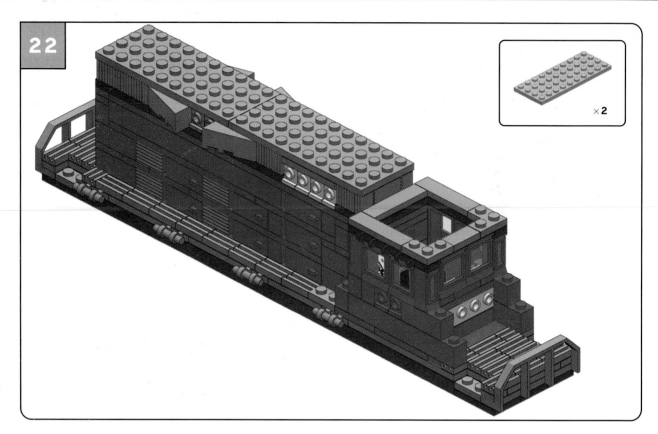

×2

23

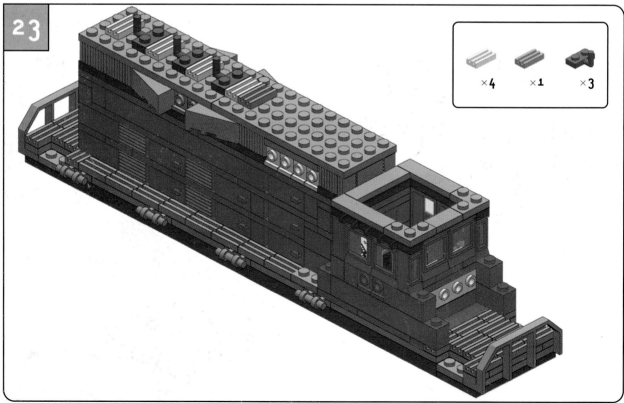

×4   ×1   ×3

24

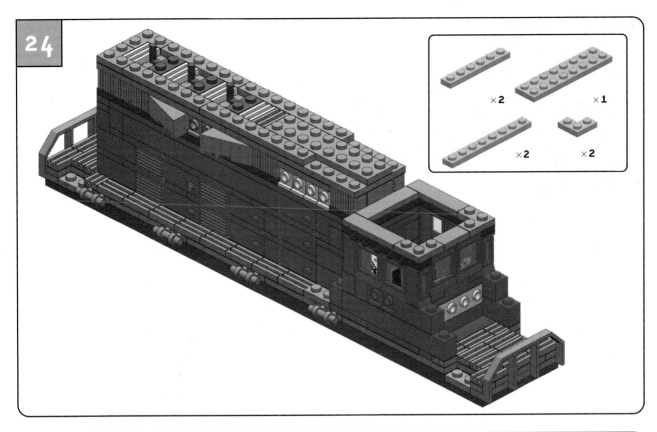

×2 ×1 ×2 ×2

25

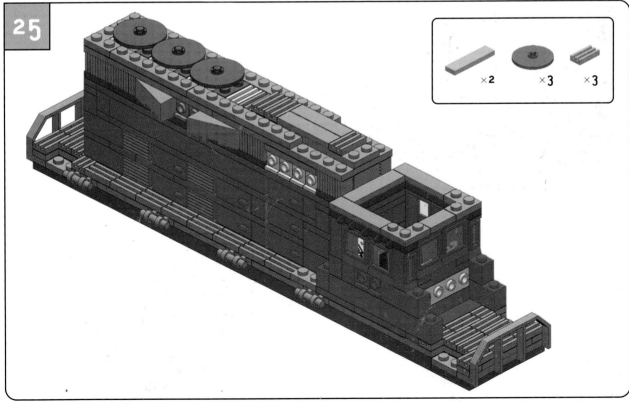

×2 ×3 ×3

26

×2   ×6   ×4

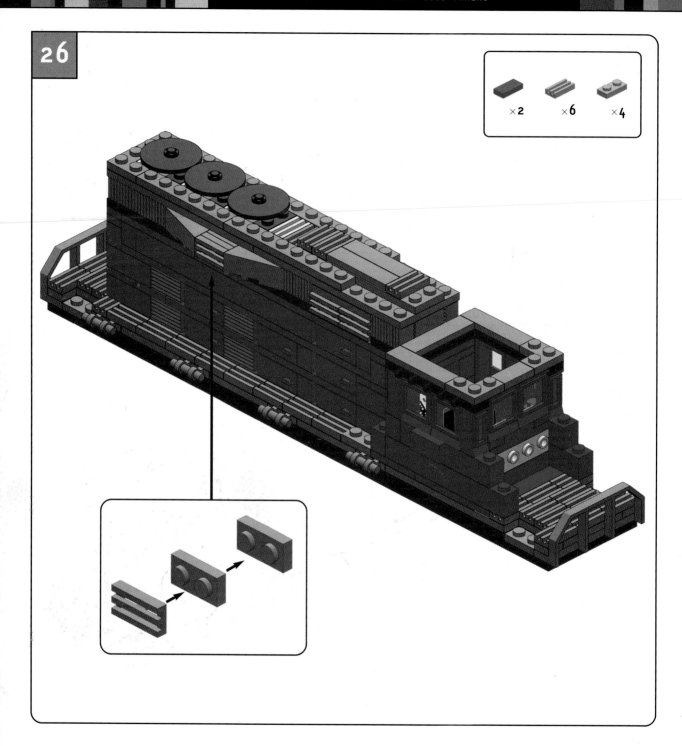

27

×2   ×8

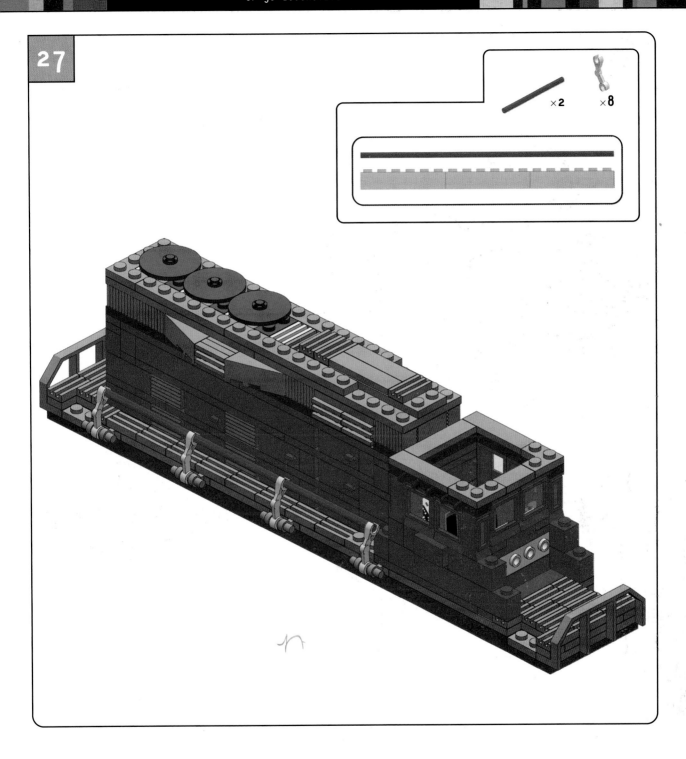

28

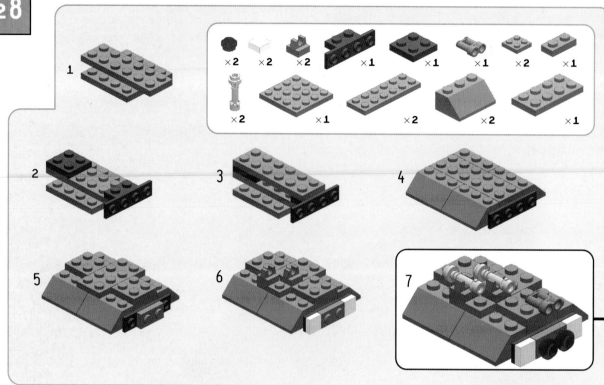

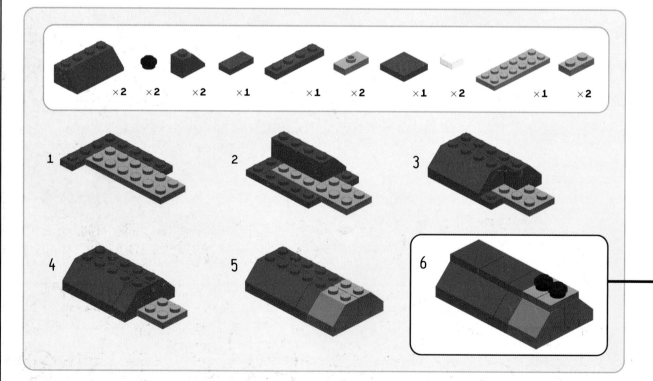

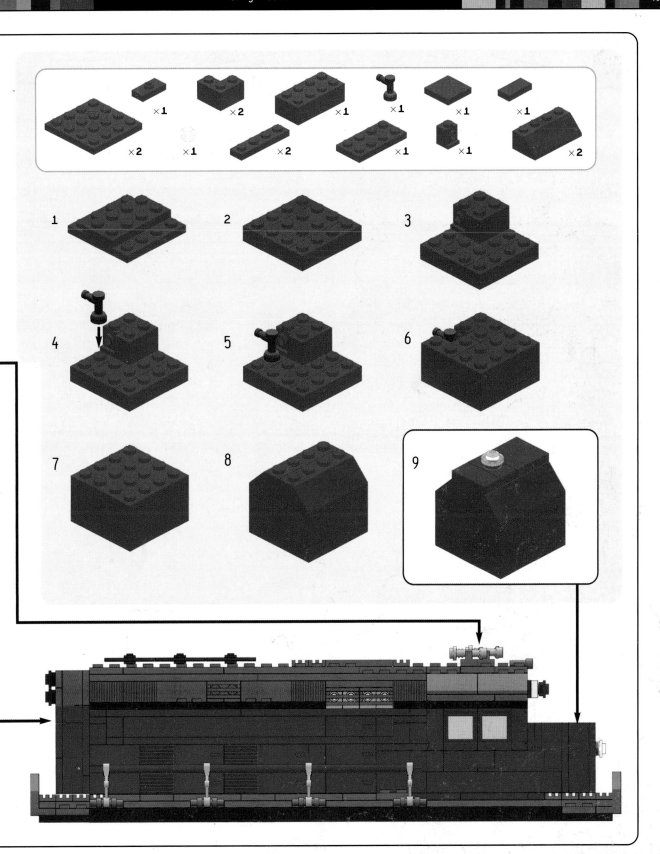

29

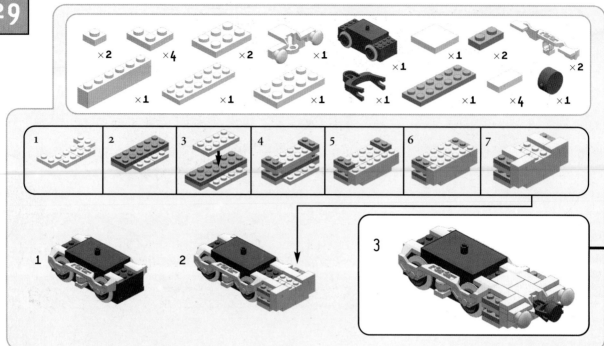

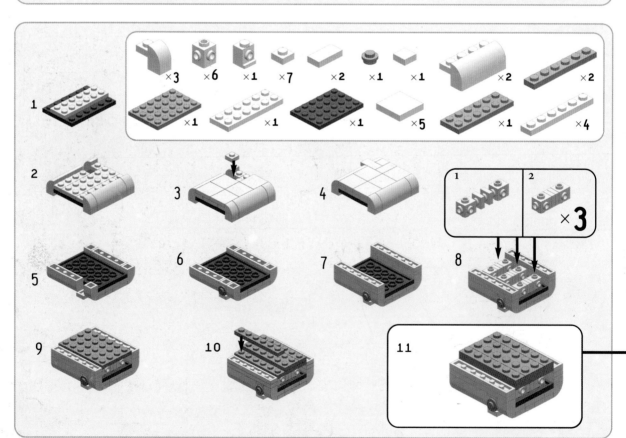

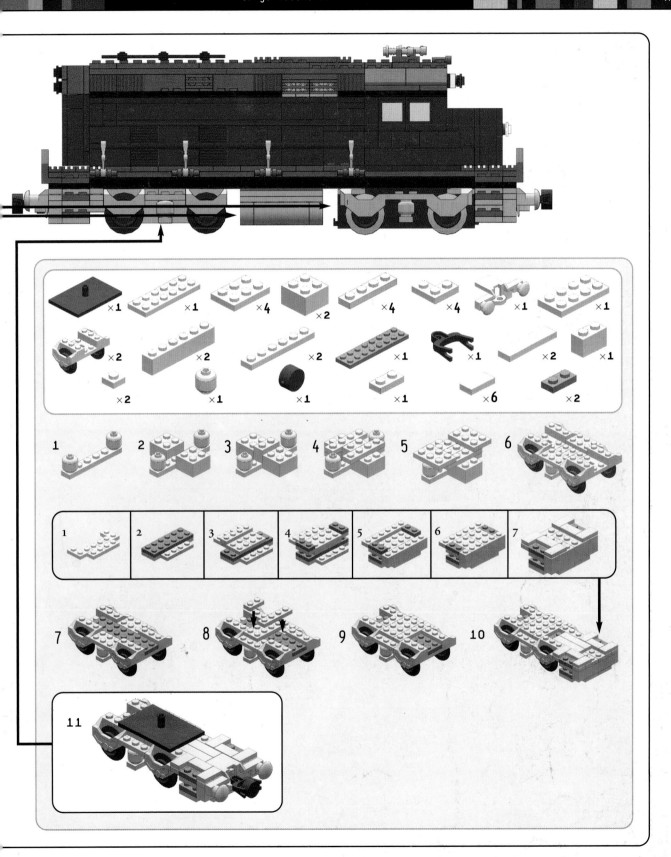

30

CHAPTER 5

OLD-STYLE REFRIGERATOR CAR

Since the early days of the railroads, large amounts of food have moved around the country in refrigerated rail cars. Today's cars use mechanical refrigeration units, but prior to their development, ice had to be used in these *reefer* cars (short for "refrigerated") to keep the food cool. Hundreds, perhaps thousands, of these cars used to rumble down the tracks delivering fresh produce, meats, and other perishable goods to markets around the country.

Over the years, these wooden reefers were continually upgraded to improve the effectiveness of the ice cooling. Still, the thing about ice is that it melts. Every so often, the train had to stop at icing stations along the track to replace the melted ice. The fresh ice was added to the reefer cars through openings in their roofs.

This old-style reefer car was one of my favorite LEGO models so far. (Figure 1)

Using the Internet and the LEGO CAD software (see www.ldraw.org for more info on the software), fellow LEGO Train builder James Mathis and I collaborated on this design. Together we developed a ter-

rific design that, while simple, is still quite elegant.

COLOR SCHEME
The great thing about reefers is that thousands were built over the years. Many were owned by companies who branded them with their colors and logos in order to use them as moving billboards. The result is that there are easily hun-

dreds of different color schemes, which means that you can either find photos of real cars that you like and match their colors, or just choose a color scheme that you like.

This particular LEGO model was originally built in a brown color scheme, but after we finalized the design, I built the version in sand green, which is shown here. As the theory goes, if you create a great design, it doesn't look good in only one color—it looks great in multiple colors. The challenge then is to find just the right color scheme—the color scheme that you like the best.

The design of this model is fairly straightforward, but of course, even the simplest designs have their share of challenges, and this model was no exception. But in the end, we created a simple design that really comes alive because of its simple details.

→ **NOTE**: *As with the locomotive model, there are complete building instructions for this model at the end of this chapter. In this chapter, we will also outline some key detailing techniques that you will be able to use in other models you build.*

DESIGNING THE TRAIN CAR

Let's jump into the design of this car. As with the locomotive model from the last chapter, there are complete building instructions at the end of this chapter. In order to help understand the design decisions a little better, we will focus on some specific design elements.

CAR BODY
Overall Body Structure

The basic design of the car body is quite simple. Using the "cross your lines" technique described in Chapter 4, we built up the main structure of the body. The body of this car is basically a standard rectangle.

To add some visual interest to the body, I used the same 1×2 corrugated brick technique used in the locomotive. This created the look of venting.

To add additional texture and details, attach two 1×1 headlight bricks next to each other, as shown. This SNOT technique allows you to fasten a 1×2 grille tile to the side of the body to replicate another type of vent. These details help to break up the solid color body. (Figures 2 – 5)

Ladder Detail

Most boxcars have ladders that run up the sides of the car to allow the train crew to climb to the roof and inspect the cars. In the case of wooden reefers, these ladders also allowed the train crew to access the ice hatches.

To replicate these ladders, I used the standard ladder element. I had hoped to use ladders and doors that were the same color as the body of the reefer to provide more realism, but LEGO doesn't make sand-green ladders yet. Instead, I substituted dark-gray ladders

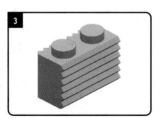

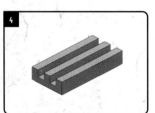

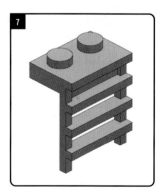

and black doors, each readily available in current sets.

When building with LEGO, it is important to find ways to work around challenges. Not being able to find parts in the right colors can require a color replacement or even a redesign. In this case, the color change actually helps make the design look more interesting. (Figures 6 – 8)

Reefer Car Endcaps

On a real reefer, the ends of the car were painted a darker color than the rest of the car body. This coloring was a key design element to replicate. But if normal construction techniques were used to create the endcaps, with all the studs pointing up, the black coloring would take up too much of the end of the train—a full brick's width. That certainly wouldn't do.

To work around this design challenge, SNOT techniques were used to create an endcap that allows the black coloring to stay only on the end of the car. Of the three-plate-thick endcap, the bottom two layers match the color of the main car body. The top layer of the endcap is black. (Figures 9 – 11)

Endcap Detailing

The endcaps offer a huge opportunity to really make the design pop by adding just a few minor details.

The key here is not to add realism as much as to represent realism. Adding three 1×2 panel parts helps to represent steps of ladder.

You can create the look of a fan with the base of a 2×2 turntable. Since the turntable part is actually two pieces, you have to separate the two pieces. Simply pop the light-gray part out of the base.

To finish up the endcap details, fill in the empty spots with 1×2 grille tiles.

Attach Endcaps

The ends of the car have used 1×4 bricks with studs on the top and one side to allow the endcap to be attached to the car. As you can see, the endcap can now attach at 90 degrees. (Figures 12 & 13)

ROOF

Removable Roof

Since this car has great interior detail, it was very important to make the roof removable to add to the car's playability. To do so, we decided to use tiles, rather than plates along the top of the train car where the roof would normally attach to the car. This ensures that the roof will simply rest in place, since the tiles don't have studs for the roof to lock onto.

As you can see in the building instructions, the roof is sturdily built. It has to be strong enough to stay in one piece when you remove or replace it on the model. (Figures 14 & 15)

Roof Ribbing

The older reefer car roofs had a "rib" design. The ribs were pieces of metal that extended across the top of the roof. This helped to add strength to the real-world roof. In our model,

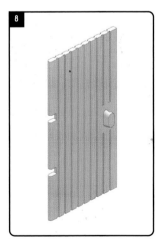

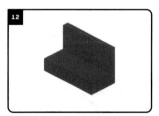

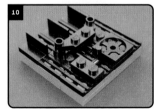

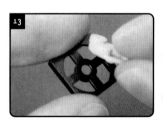

it just adds a great effect. This is a distinct design element, so we had to include it in our model.

To recreate this ribbing, we first divided the roof into sections to make sure that we got the right spacing between ribs. For this design, the roof can be divided into five sections, as shown in the building instructions. These five sections are each four studs wide. In each of these five sections, 3×4 33° slopes create a majority of the roof. Between each of these five sections, leave a one stud gap. These gaps are filled in with a 1x6 plate, then on top of the plates, 3×1 33° slopes. These 3×1 33° slopes form the "ribs" because they are elevated one plate above the 3×4 33° slopes. (Figures 16 – 18)

Ice Hatch Doors

When reefers used ice to cool the cargo, train crews used doors in the roof, located directly above the ice bins, to load in new ice.

On our model, these doors are built into the removable roof. In the end sections described previously, we forgo the 3×4 33° slopes for 1×4 hinge plates and train gates.

Roof Walkways

Like most old train cars, reefers had walkways across the top of the roof that allowed train crews to walk along the top of the train while in motion.

To produce a realistic looking walkway, use 1×2 grille tiles. Standard plates wouldn't have looked quite right because they

looked too smooth. The real train walkways couldn't be smooth metal or the train crew would have slipped right off. (Figures 21 & 22)

Floating Roof Ends

The ice hatch doors add to the model's realism, and the fact that they are built into the removable roof helps make the roof more stable. But we can't stop there — the roof wouldn't look right if it ended with the folding hatches. So we need to add small endcaps in order to finalize the roof design.

These roof ends should extend to the end of the car, but since the ends of the cars are SNOT construction, there aren't any studs to attach the entire roof end to. As you can see in the image, the roof ends are two

studs wide. They are constructed to attach to one stud and float over the other stud width at the end of the car. These floating roof ends will be permanently attached and not removable.

Even though the roof ends float the width of a stud, they are close enough to the SNOT end-caps to support the roof ends. (Figures 23 & 24)

Interior Details

On the actual train cars, beneath the ice hatch doors, the reefer cars had ice bins to hold the blocks of ice. This model includes a representation of those ice bins.

Although our designs don't look exactly like the real ice bins, they are close enough, and

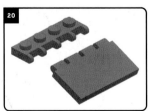

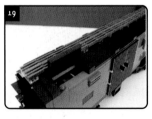

they use a basic design. I've added clear white and clear blue 1×1 round plates to represent ice.

Originally, I had hoped to make the bins brown, to represent wood. However, I had a hard time finding the right parts and instead chose light gray. (Figure 25)

Undercarriage

The important part of designing LEGO models is to create the basic look of a model or part of a model, not to design it as an exact replica. Like the ice bins, the undercarriage replicates a few important details and adopts a basic design to convey the feel of the real-world undercarriage.

This subassembly uses basic SNOT techniques to put the steps in the right position. The building instructions showcase the construction methods. (Figure 26)

Trucks

The key element of the trucks is the step design. Borrowing a technique from the LEGO Super Chief cars designed by fan James Mathis, the trucks use a subassembly turned upside down and held in place with a 1×4 plate with arm. (Figure 27)

Cargo

To finish off this model, you can add cargo. Using the common LEGO crates and fruit, as well as some 1×1 cone bricks, you can easily create a full load. After all, what's a reefer car without something to refrigerate? (Figure 28)

Take a stab at tweaking this design. You can easily modify it to take on the look of a modern steel design, or of other styles of boxcars.

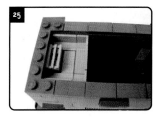

Alternative Color Schemes

AS WITH MOST LEGO MODELS, YOU CAN CREATE A "NEW" MODEL SIMPLY BY CHANGING THE COLOR SCHEME. DURING THE DESIGN PROCESS, I BUILT MODELS USING THE COLORS SAND GREEN, BROWN, RED, EARTH ORANGE, AND YELLOW.

ON A REAL RAILROAD, MANY COLOR SCHEMES OF THE SAME TYPE OF TRAIN CAR OFTEN MAKE UP A FULL TRAIN. TRY A FEW COLOR COMBINATIONS ON YOUR OWN AND CREATE A FULL TRAIN OF REEFER CARS.

1

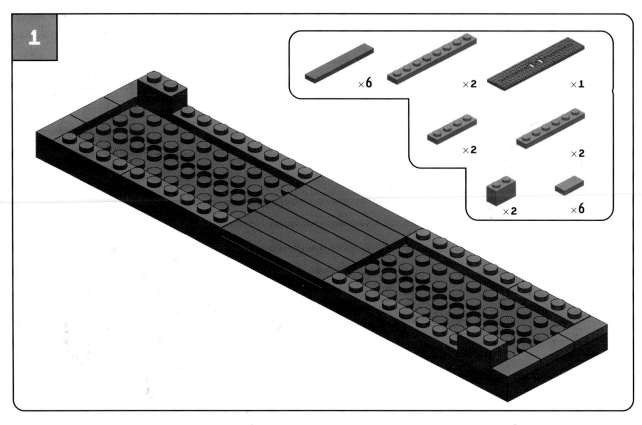

2

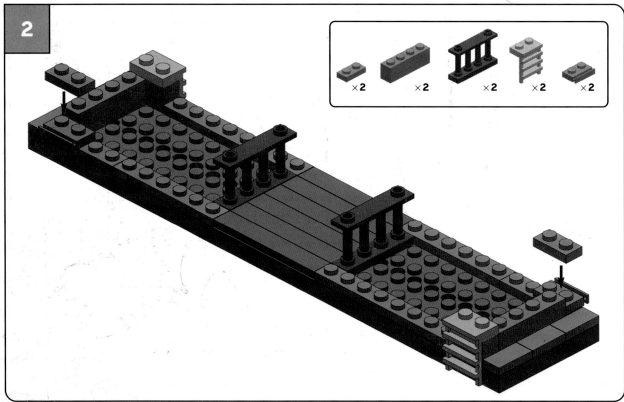

3

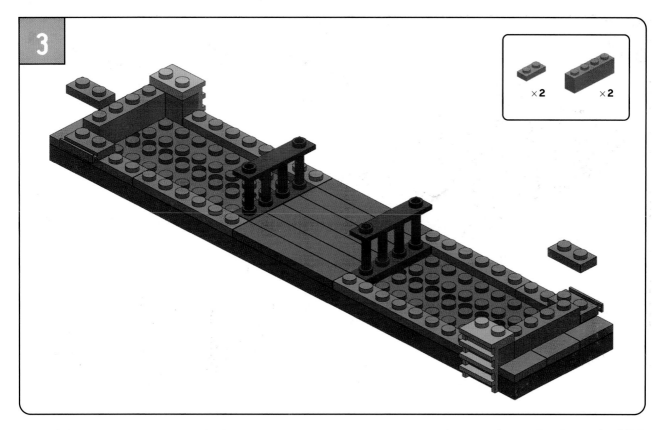

4

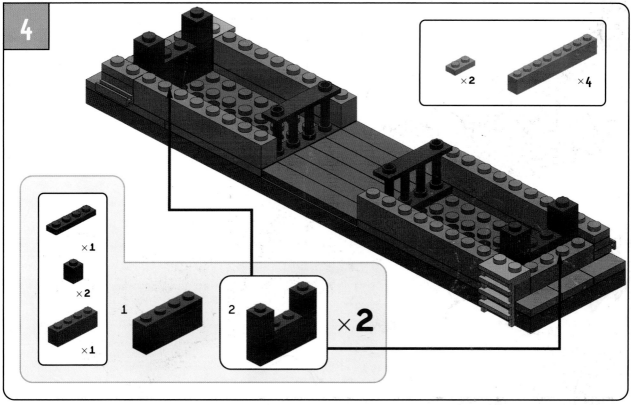

5

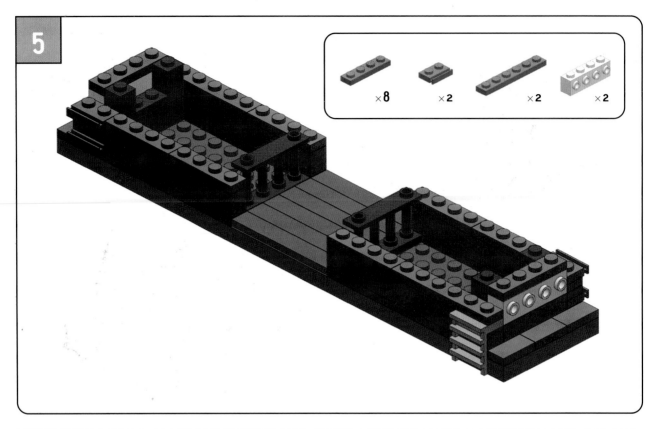

×8   ×2   ×2   ×2

6

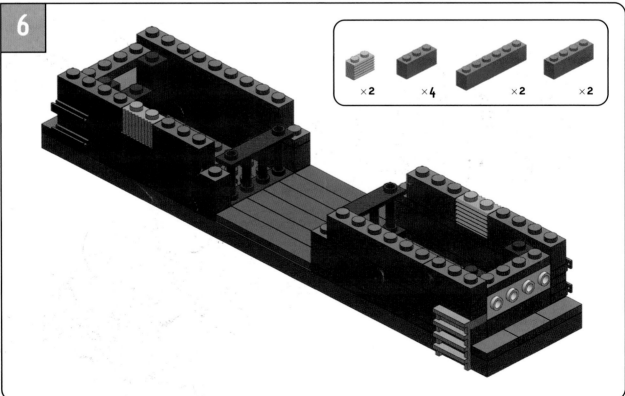

×2   ×4   ×2   ×2

7

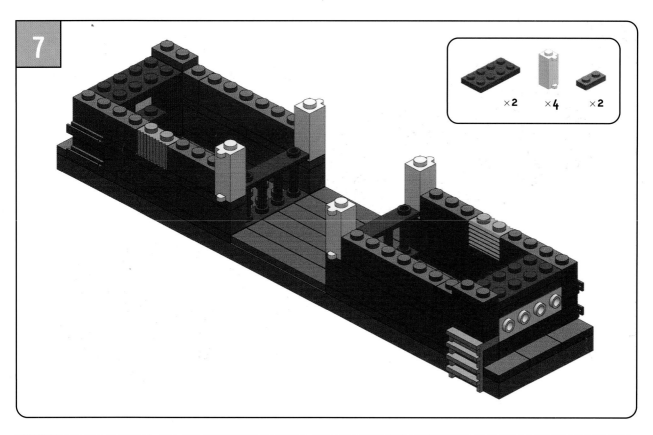

×2 ×4 ×2

8

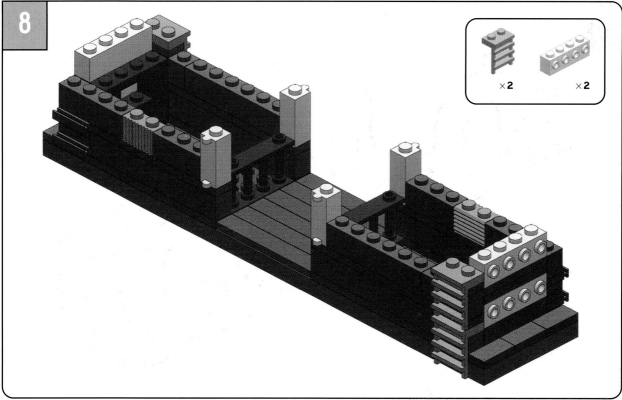

×2 ×2

9

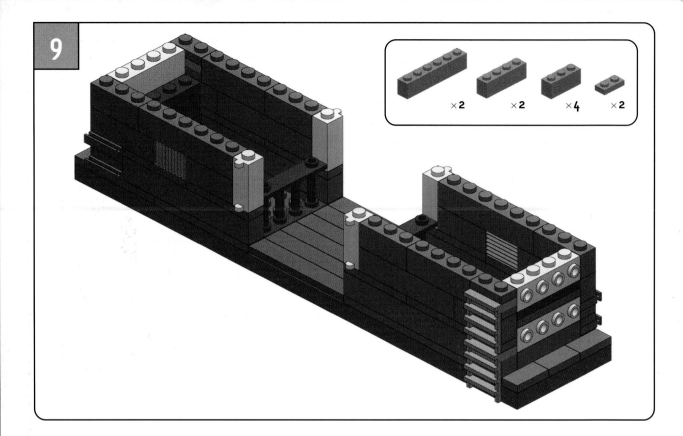

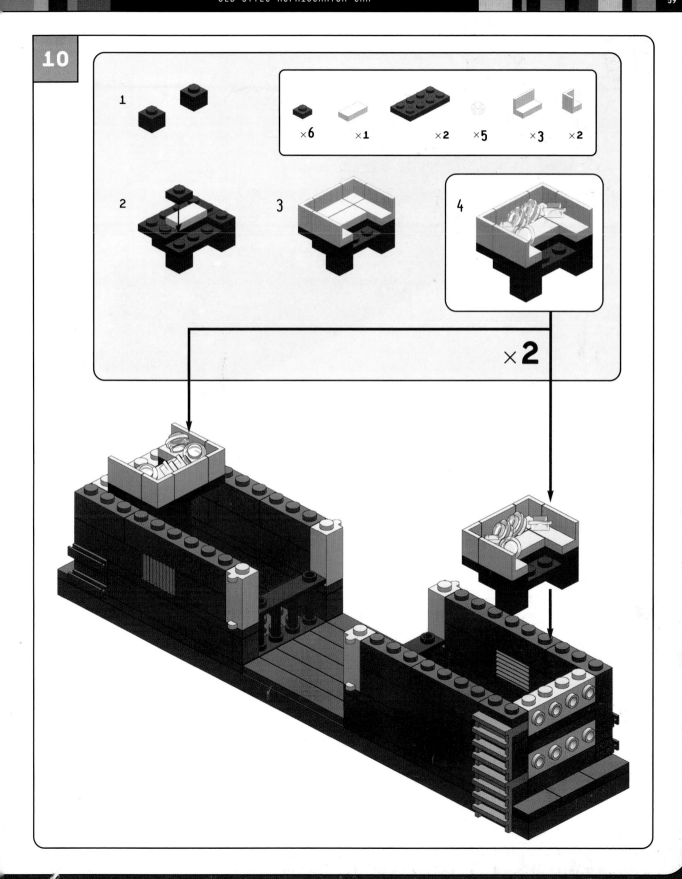

11

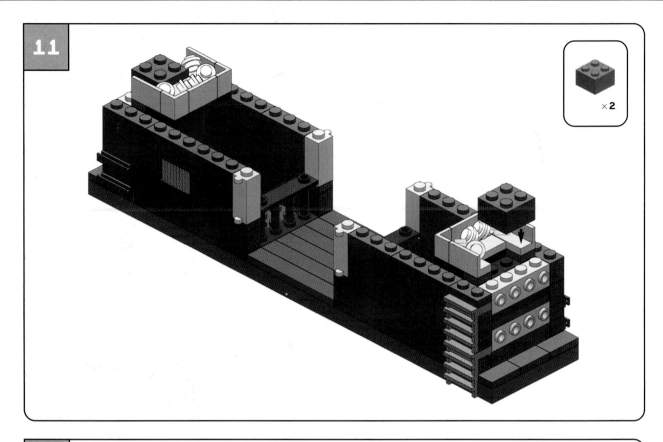

12

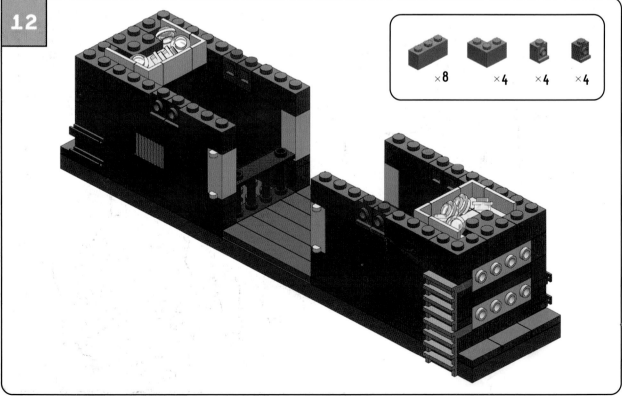

13

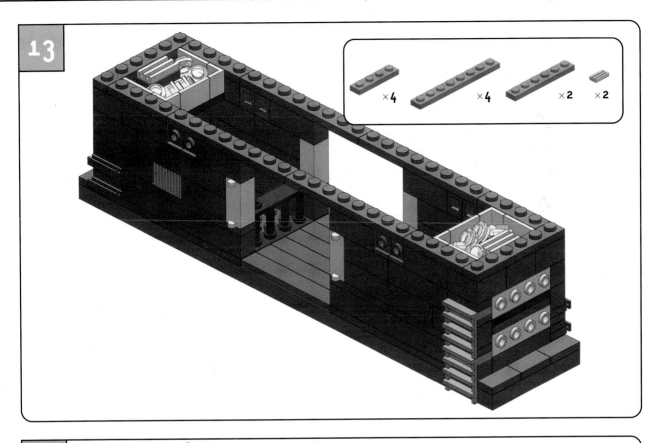

×4 ×4 ×2 ×2

14

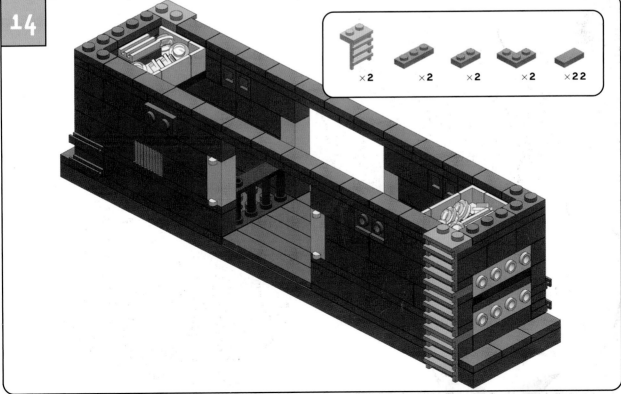

×2 ×2 ×2 ×2 ×22

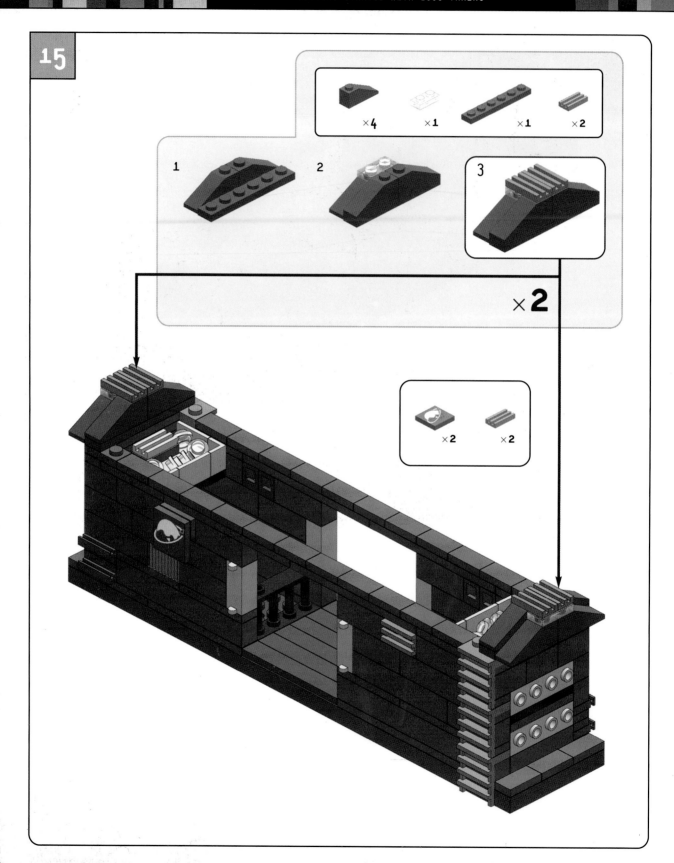

16

×**4**

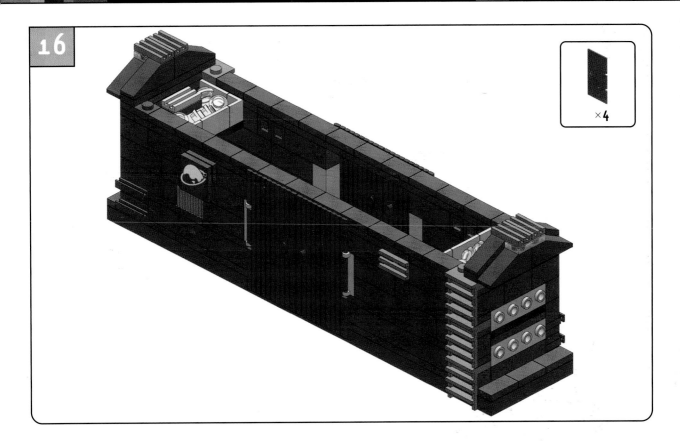

17

1

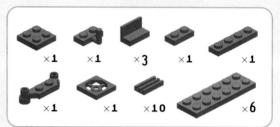

×1 ×1 ×3 ×1 ×1

×1 ×1 ×10 ×6

2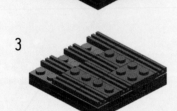

3

4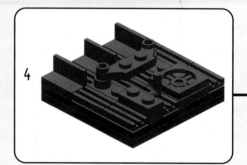

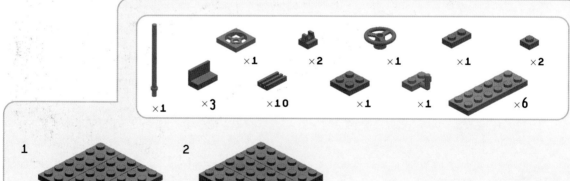

×1 ×1 ×2 ×1 ×1 ×2

×3 ×10 ×1 ×1 ×6

1 2

3 4

5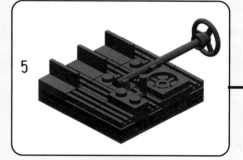

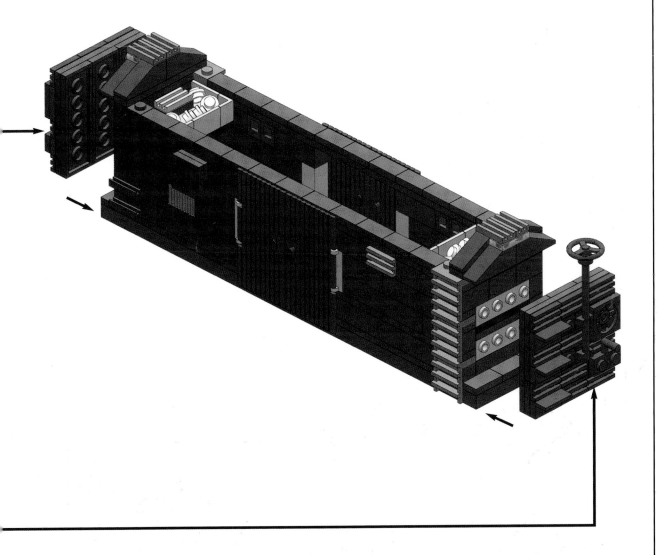

18

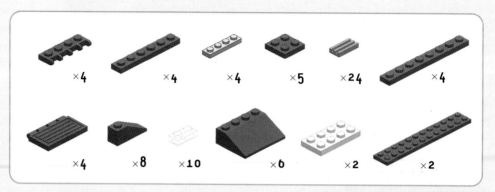

×4 ×4 ×4 ×5 ×24 ×4

×4 ×8 ×10 ×6 ×2 ×2

1

2

3

4
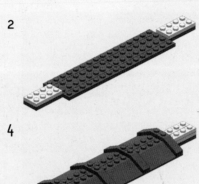

5

6

7
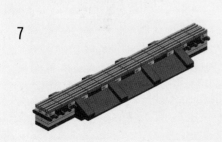

8
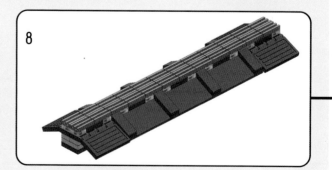

19

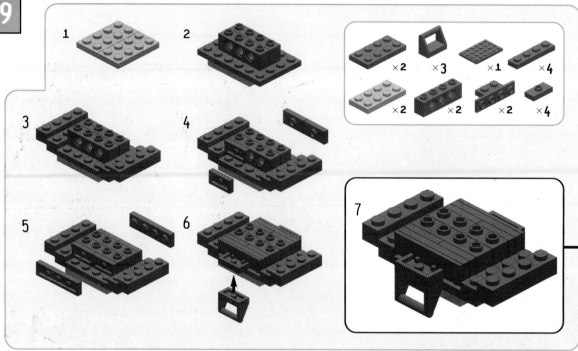

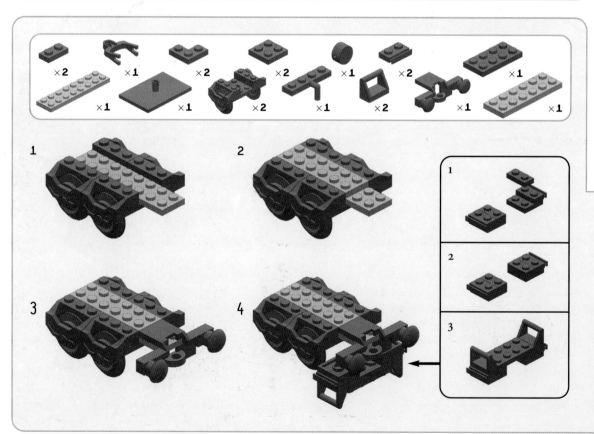

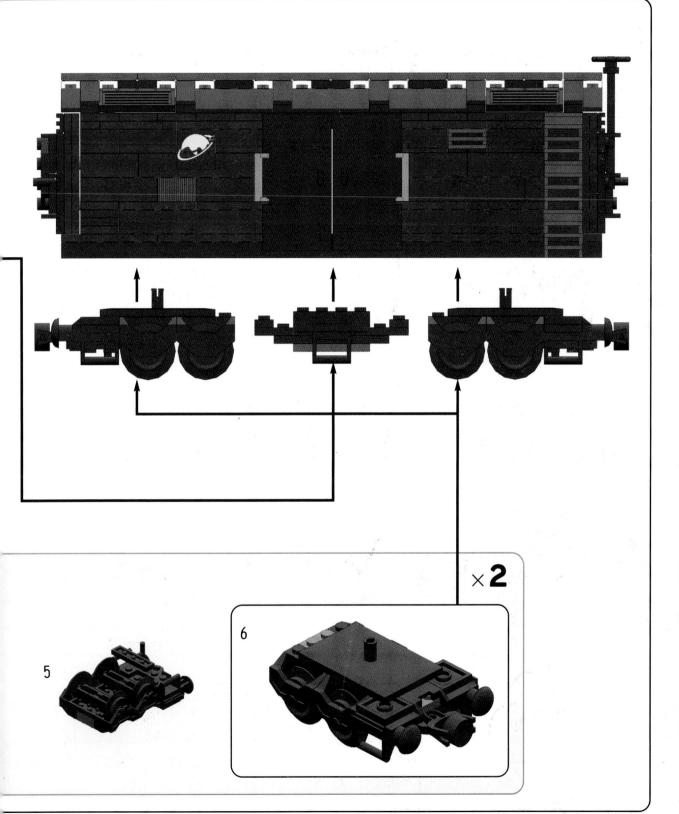

× **2**

6

5

20

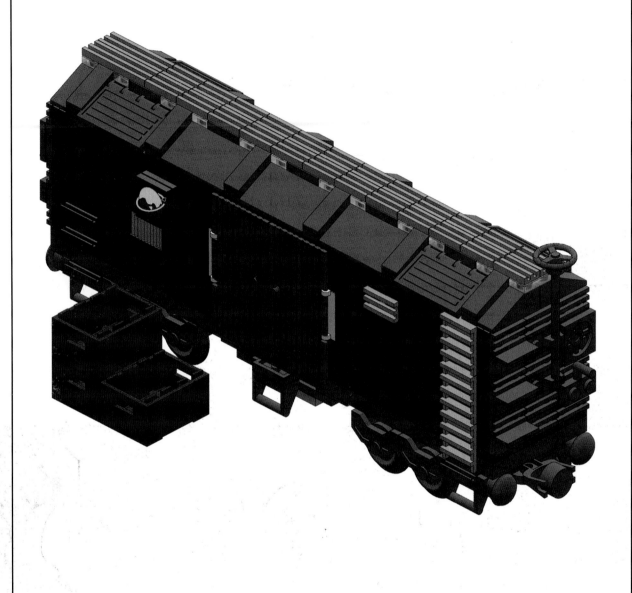

CHAPTER 6

INTERMODAL CONTAINER CAR

There was a time when everything that was shipped from one place to another had to be transferred from one vehicle to another. For instance, goods would come off a ship and then be moved into a train car. Then from the train car, they would be moved onto a truck. Each time the goods were moved, they could easily be damaged. To solve this problem, *intermodal* (meaning multiple method) shipping containers were invented. When a manufacturer creates goods today, they are placed directly into a shipping container, nice and tight so that nothing gets damaged. This container remains packed until it reaches its final destination—the entire container is moved from ship to train to truck.

The containers are standard sizes, so that they can be easily moved from any container ship to any container train car to any container trailer. Using the standard locking mechanism built into each container, a truck, ship, and freight train can all lock down the container the same way.

You've almost certainly seen a container en route, either on a freight train or pulled by a semi truck. You know those colorful semi trailers with names like Evergreen, Hyundai, or Maersk? Those are containers.

For this last model, we are going to build an *intermodal well car* (also known as a *stack* or *double stack car*). These cars are quite common on North American railroads today and can be seen in a variety of colors. Keep an eye out for them. These container cars, and trains made up of many container cars, are quickly becoming one of the most common types of cars on railroads.

Well cars typically carry two long containers stacked one on top of the other. Smaller containers are sometimes used instead of the full-size, long containers. These are half the length of their full-size counterparts. Containers can be stacked on top of each other and locked in place—container cars can carry two containers stacked on top of each other. Any higher than two, though, and the cars couldn't go through tunnels or under bridges.

There are two common sizes of containers: a full container that is the length of a standard semi trailer, and a short container that is half the length of the full container. Container cars can carry up to four containers each—two full containers, or four short containers, or one full container and two short containers. (Figure 1)

These container train cars can be seen in a number of solid colors. For our model, we'll use the most common yellow design.

As you will see when you build the model, this model doesn't use the standard train base plate that our first two models did. The reason for this is that the real intermodal cars don't have a solid floor. Since large containers are the only item

that these cars transport, the car is really just a frame to carry these containers. You can see straight through the car to the ground. (This saves money because less metal is used in the car, and the cars don't collect dirt and grime as easily.)

As with the previous models, full building instructions for this model are provided at the end of this chapter.

BASIC CONSTRUCTION

One of the best things about using the standard train base plate is that it makes the overall structure of the train car much more stabile. As you add parts or play with models, the base plate absorbs much of the downward force.

Since this model does not use the base plate, I needed to make sure that the structure of this model was robust enough to allow the car to be played with. Since this model encourages builders to load containers on

and off, I needed to make sure that when containers were pushed down onto the car, the car didn't fall apart.

I used two main side walls and added some basic cross members to form the main body of the car. To create these cross members, I connected four 1×6 plates to the two side walls.

This may, at first, seem somewhat unstable, because the cross members are sandwiched between two layers of bricks, but it turns out to be pretty solid. Also, both ends of the cars are built to eliminate side-to-side movement, which adds more stability. (Figure 2)

One major problem with my original design of this car was that the ends of the car and the open bottom area separated if even light pressure was applied to the top of the car. To help eliminate this problem, I added a Z-shaped bracket to better connect the car end with the

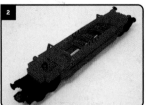

car side rails. This Z shape helped hold the ends of the cars together with the side walls. (Figures 3 & 4)

CONTAINER PLACEMENT HEIGHT

As you build this car, you will see how important the cross members are. They not only hold the two side walls together; they also provide a place to rest the containers when they are set on the car.

However, because the containers are placed directly on the black cross members, they sit too low and don't look quite right. Since we can't easily move the black strip up, we need to create risers to elevate the containers.

As you can see in the image, these risers are pretty basic, but they get the job done. An extra couple of plates and we are back in business. Remember, there are always multiple ways to solve any problem. (Figure 5)

TOPSIDE DETAILS

Details are what make your models come alive. As with the reefer car model, a few subtle details really add a lot to this train car.

On each end of the car, I added air tanks and a brake wheel to produce a greater feeling of realism. Additionally, by adding 1×2 tiles with handles, you can add a bit of a split between the "well" area where the containers sit and the "deck" area where the crew would walk. (Figures 6 & 7)

ATTACHING WHEELSETS

Because this design doesn't use the standard train base plate, we need to find some other way to attach the wheelsets to the car. The easiest way is to use a 2×4 TECHNIC plate because the holes in that plate are the same size as those in the train base plate.

The key to using the TECHNIC plate to attach the wheelsets is to ensure that there is not another brick or plate directly above the hole. The pin on top of the wheelsets needs to have at least a one-plate area directly above the hole free in order to allow the pin to attach to the plate. (Figures 8 & 9)

Intermodal cars are typically grouped in sets of three or five individual cars, and these groups are referred to as single cars by the railroads. These "single" cars are articulated, meaning that they share wheelsets. When we talk about wheelset sharing, what we mean is that the

car bodies share wheelsets between two car bodies. This "joins" two cars together to make one "single" car.

You can easily create an articulated version of this model simply by building multiple copies of it and joining them with shared wheelsets. Use the standard wheelsets on both far ends of the "single" car, and use the shared truck wheelsets between cars . (For more information on articulated cars, see the sidebar.) (Figure 10)

CONTAINER DESIGN

The containers for this train car are based on the standard LEGO design used in a number of older sets. (For more information on which sets, visit www.bricksonthebrain.com/trains.)

These containers follow a standard and very effective design. You should be able to construct them easily by following the building instructions.

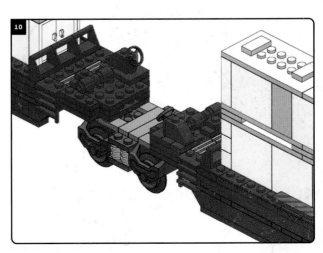

As you can see from the image, you can use two different types of doors to design containers. One style uses doors that are contained within the 1×4×3 window frame part. The other style uses doors (window shutters, actually) that attach on the outside of another style of 1×4×3 window frame part. This second type has a small nub that is used to hold the doors (shutters).

If you choose to use the window frame with the doors (shutters) located on the outside (marked as B in the image), you will need to move the 1×2 tile with handle parts (three on each end of the car) away from the containers by one stud. The window frame attaches the doors (shutters) on the outside of the frame with small nubs that don't fit into the standard design. (Figures 11–14)

Articulated Intermodal Train Cars

AS DISCUSSED EARLIER, AN ARTICULATED INTERMODAL TRAIN CAR IS A SERIES OF INTERMODAL TRAIN CARS THAT SHARE WHEELSETS. ARTICULATED INTERMODAL WELL CARS ARE TYPICALLY FOUND IN GROUPS OF EITHER THREE OR FIVE CAR SETS.

EACH CAR IS REFERRED TO BY A "SUB-LETTER"—A SINGLE LETTER THAT IDENTIFIES THE CAR. THE LETTER A IS GIVEN TO THE FIRST CAR, B TO THE LAST, AND THE OTHER LETTERS ARE FILLED IN WORKING FROM THE END OF THE GROUP TO THE FRONT:

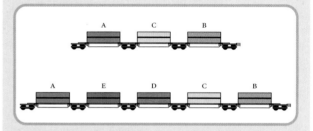

ARTICULATED TRAIN CARS OFFER SEVERAL ADVANTAGES OVER STANDARD TRAIN CARS. SINCE THE ARTICULATED CARS USE FEWER TRUCKS, THEY REDUCE THE WEIGHT OF THE TRAIN, AND LIGHTER TRAINS ARE CHEAPER TO OPERATE. ALSO, BECAUSE THERE ARE FEWER COUPLERS CONNECTING THE CARS TOGETHER, THE JERKING WHEN THE TRAINS STOPS AND STARTS IS GREATLY REDUCED. THIS HELPS TO ENSURE THAT CARGO ON THE TRAIN DOESN'T GET DAMAGED.

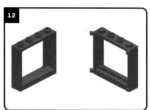

INTERVIEW WITH STEVE BARILE ON BUILDING ROLLING STOCK

Steve Barile has been building with LEGO bricks since 1970 with a brief hiatus during his teens and twenties. As an adult LEGO hobbyist, Steve is interested in all things train, including Mindstorms control and instruction publishing. He is a founding member of the Pacific Northwest LEGO Train Club (PNLTC; www.pnltc.org) and cofounder of the International LEGO Train Club Organization (www.ILTCO.org). Steve also is co-owner and designer for BricWorx (www.BricWorx.com) and is credited for coining the phrase L-gauge.

• • •

Jake: Through your work with the PNLTC and through your designs on BricWorx, you seem to build a lot of LEGO Train cars. What is your basic design process?

Steve: My design process can be described in four phases, where movement from phase to phase is triggered by inspiration and motivated by the challenge, and within each phase it tends to be iterative in nature.

Inspiration: Photos of a train or a new element color or shape—you never know what might kick off a new project.

Design: Getting down to business.

Engineering: Making sure that the train can function on the tracks.

Detailing and Finalizing: Adding details and making design tweaks. And then doing it over again. And again.

Inspiration
The first phase is to decide on a project. I love to look at color pictures of trains from my collection of train books and model railroading catalogs and magazines. Occasionally I'll use the Internet to search for trains using the image search from www.google.com.

When new colors are released by LEGO (or the assortment of rare color elements increases) the iterative process begins by poring over the train books and magazines to find examples of trains with color schemes, known as the *livery*, that match the new colors. A great example of this is the new darker colors, like dark red. The older European passenger coaches were often painted with dark reds, purples, and browns against a tan base color.

Other inspirational moments come when new element shapes are released. Then to a lesser extent when some of my fellow LEGO train friends are working on a project and invite

me to participate by designing a version of their current project; but that typically results in a critique or specific suggestions about a particular detail. However, don't underestimate the value of an honest critique by a trusted friend, or the time spent closely inspecting others' work. These are great ways to improve your skills.

Design
Next comes actually designing the model. This includes identifying the key design elements that make a particular train unique. There should be three to six elements, such as livery, truck configuration, specialty, window and door shape and count, roof line, nose shape, etc., that can be easily discernable by you and your audience. Another part of the design is choosing how to selectively scale the identified elements, or, in some cases, how to do without them. I tend to be in the camp of less-is-more, which is a delicate balancing act and sometimes can be viewed as lacking in detail. I prefer a cleaner line to a lot of gaudy embellishments.

Engineering
The third phase is the actual engineering of the train. In this way, the train theme is more of a cousin to the TECHNIC theme than to the town theme, which is typically static. Most passenger coaches and freight cars are fairly straightforward,

but there are still many great engineering challenges to be conquered in these areas. Train engines are often more challenging, especially the steam engines. Since there are no steam driver wheels for the 9 volt train series, many creative solutions are used. This is also one of the few areas where LEGO purists allow non-LEGO substitutions or even small LEGO element modifications, called *mutilations*, to slip by. There have also been some overhead railways and cog railways attempted that can be quite challenging. To finish off the engineering phase, there is also the area of animation, from simple headlights to propelled snow-blower blades, even bobbing animal heads in a circus train car.

DETAILING AND FINALIZING
Once the train project is selected, designed, and engineered, the task of detailing is at hand. It is vital to detail your creation—that is what often creates your trademark as a designer. It could often mean tearing down the entire model to fit in or add detail elements. Door knobs, inset doors, rain gutters, textures, accents, and handrails are all opportunities to customize what can otherwise look like a blob of bricks atop of a set of train wheels. This is a great area to spend time looking at what others have done. Many details have come from simple but clever

modifications of already-existing details. "If I have seen farther [than others,] it is by standing on the shoulders of giants." — Isaac Newton

Jake: Wow, what a process! How did you develop this process?

Steve: These design steps have come from six years of trying to build a collection of "the ultimate" train models. My first train was undoubtedly a blob of bricks atop a set of train wheels. Then slowly it all began to make sense. Although I enumerate the process above, it is much more an art form than construction, and like all art, it takes a ton of practice to make it look easy. Stick with it, and above all have fun with the hobby, and be supportive of others.

1

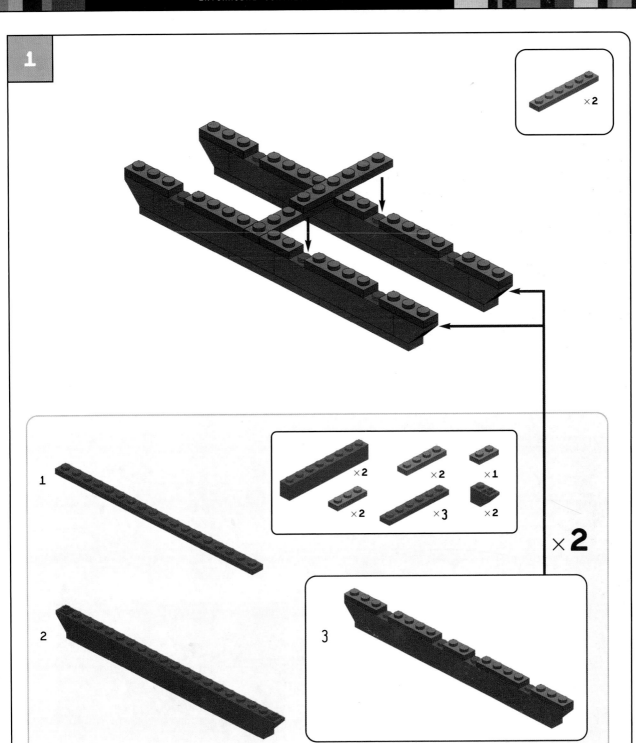

×2

1

2

3

×2
×2
×1
×2
×3
×2

×**2**

2

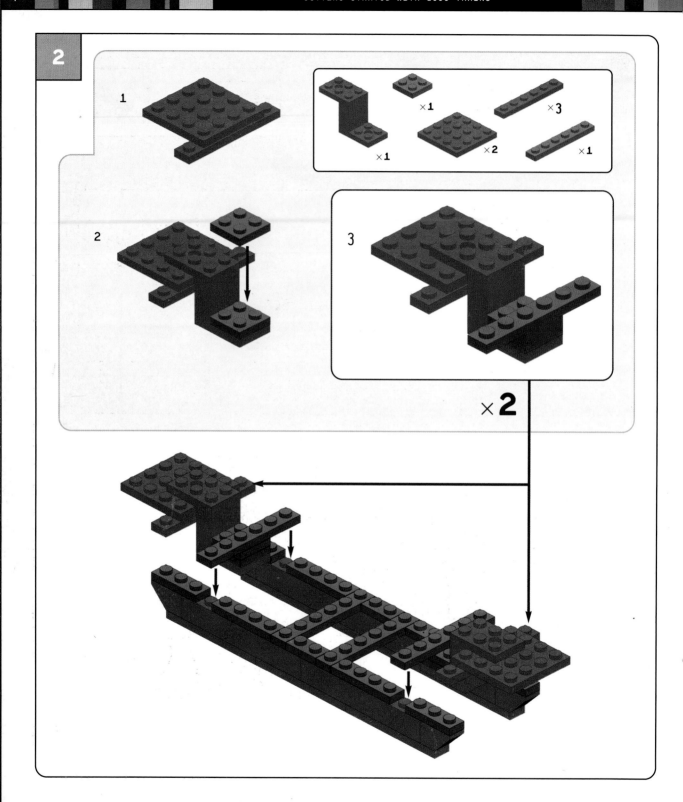

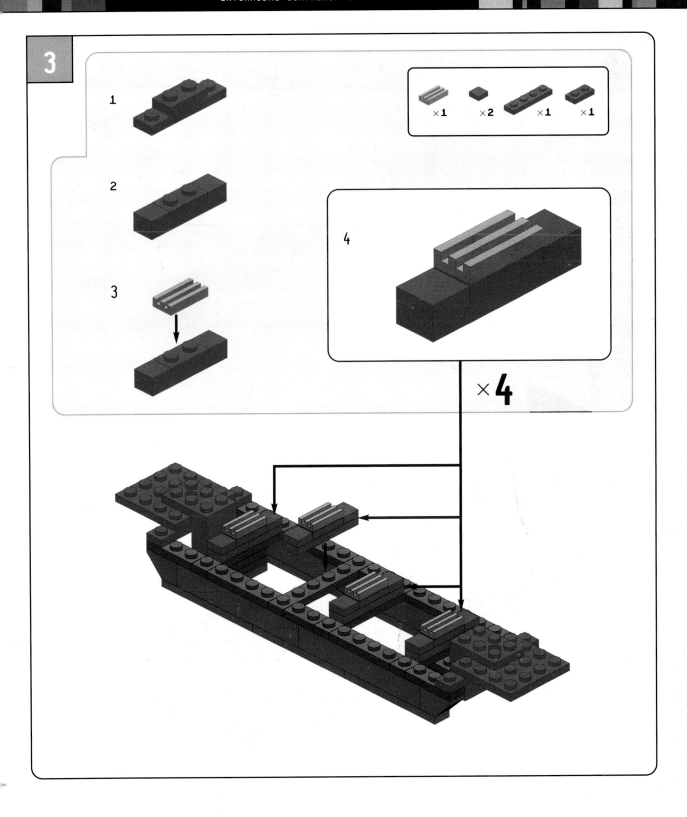

4

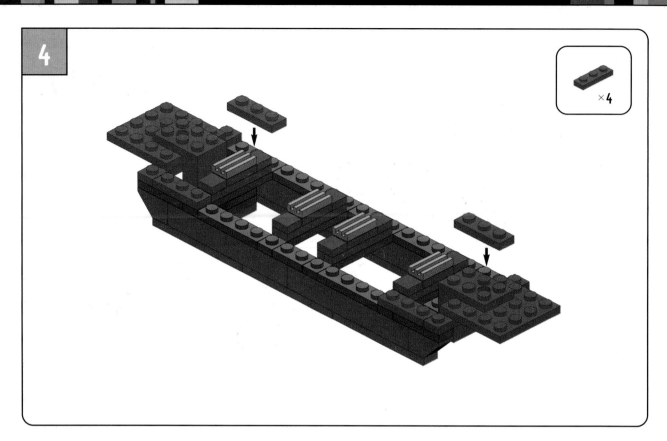

×4

5

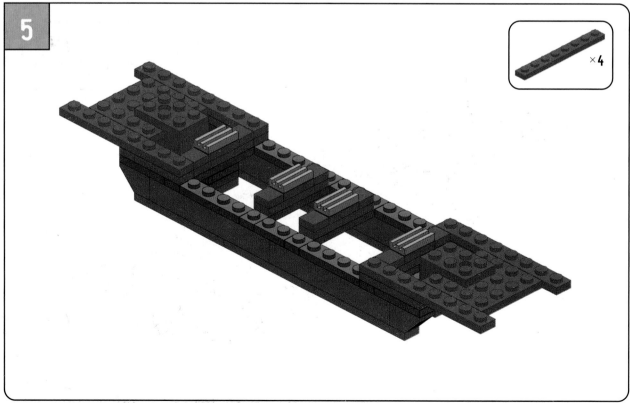

×4

6

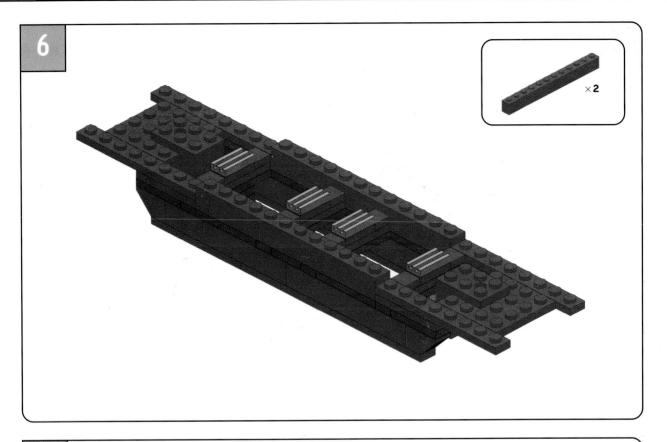

7

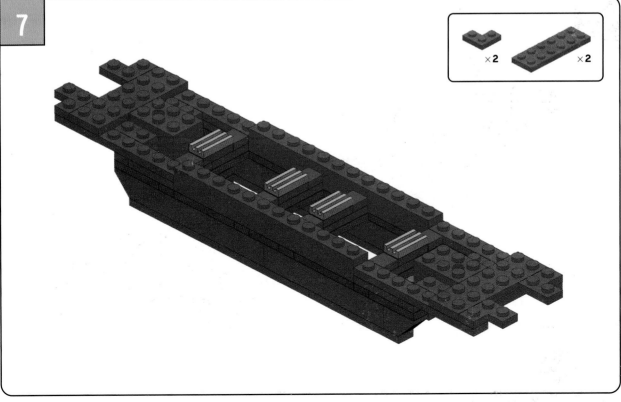

8

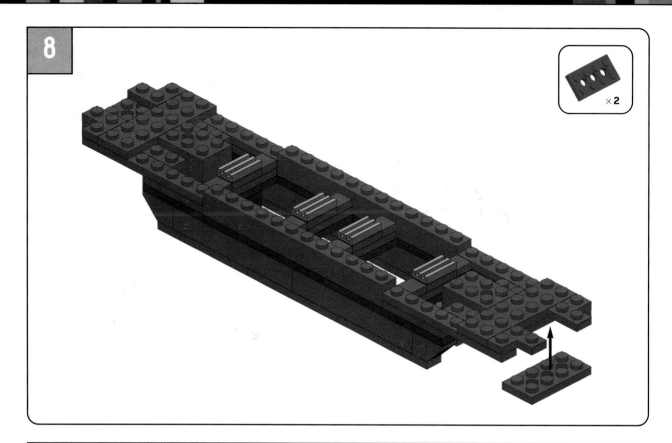

×2

9

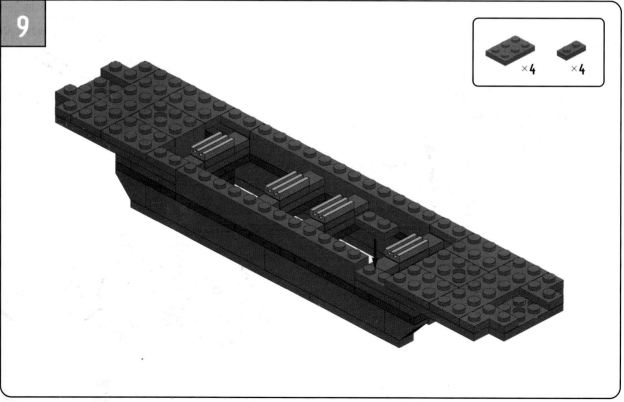

×4 ×4

10

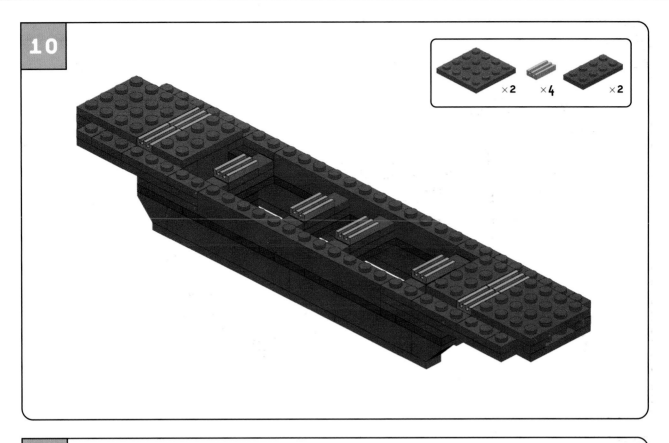

11

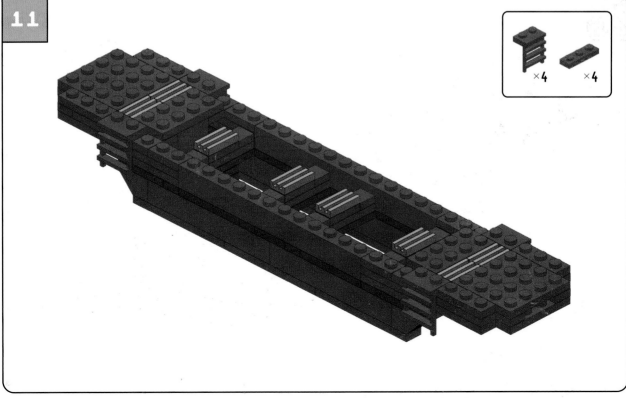

12

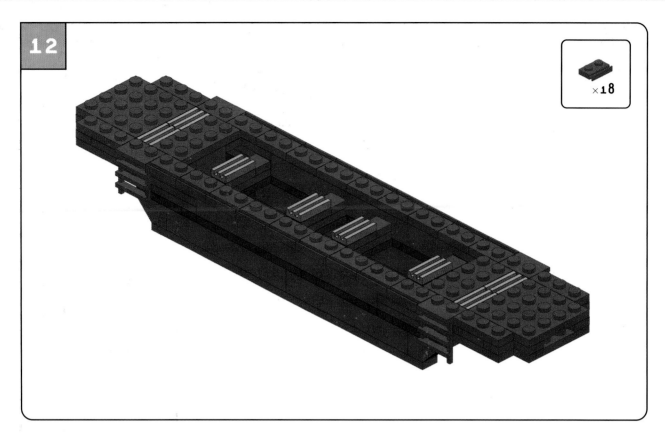

×18

13

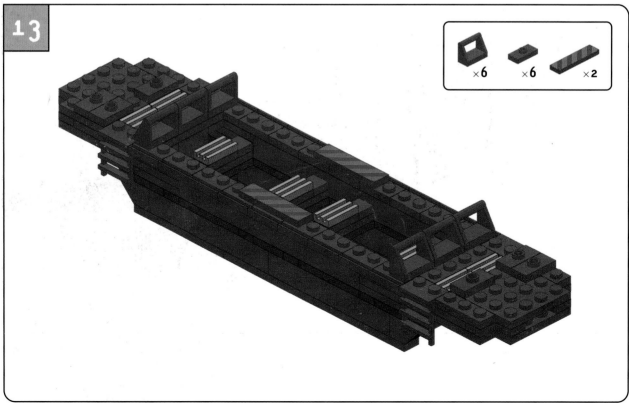

×6　×6　×2

14

1

×1   ×2

2

×**2**

×2   ×2

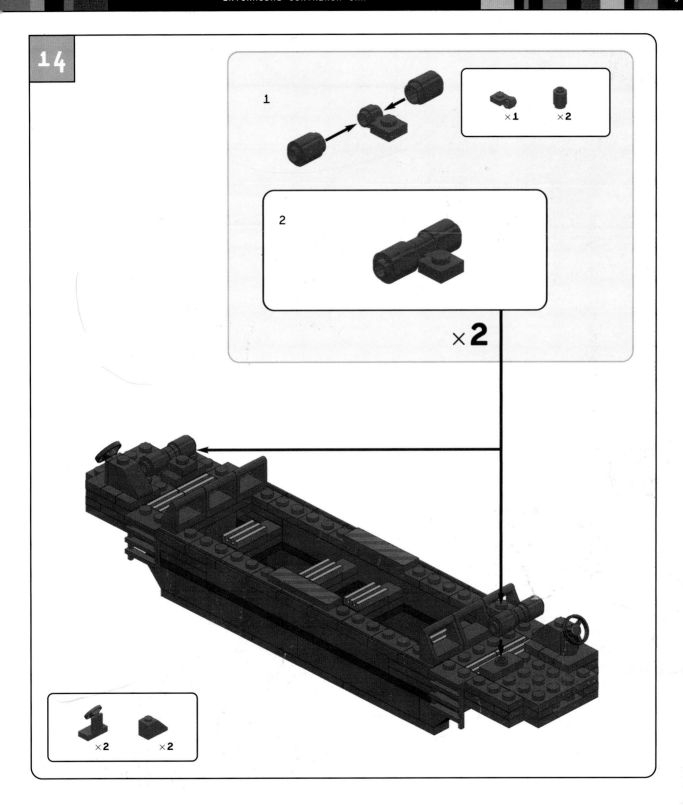

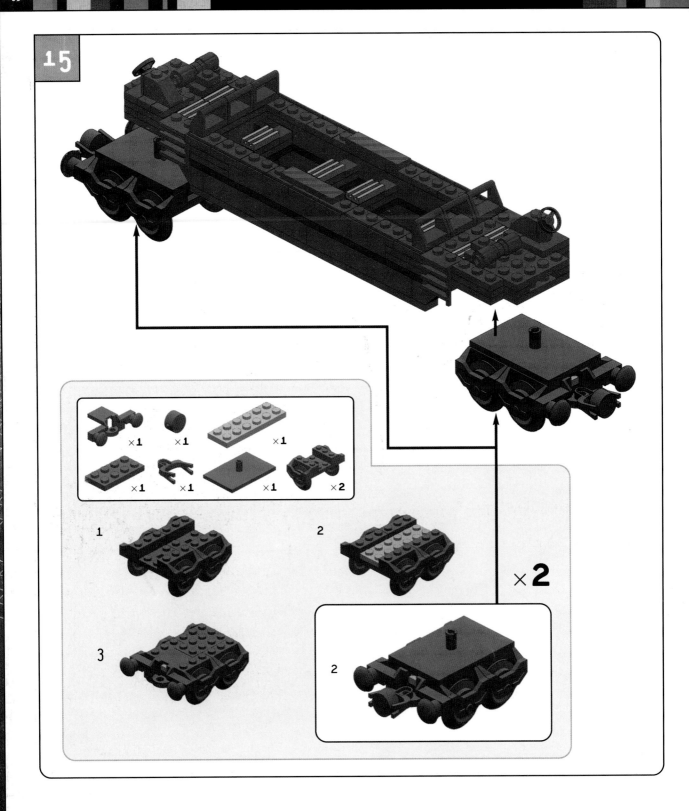

16

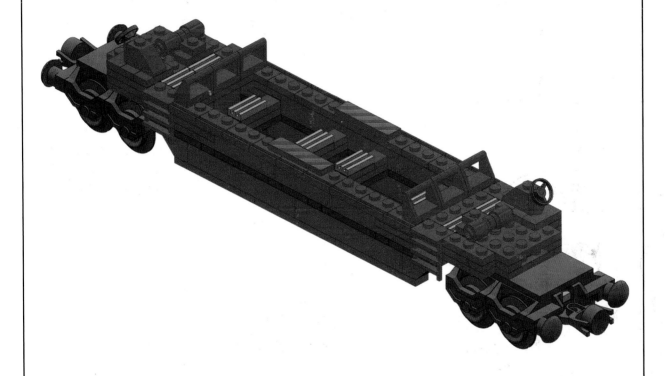

17

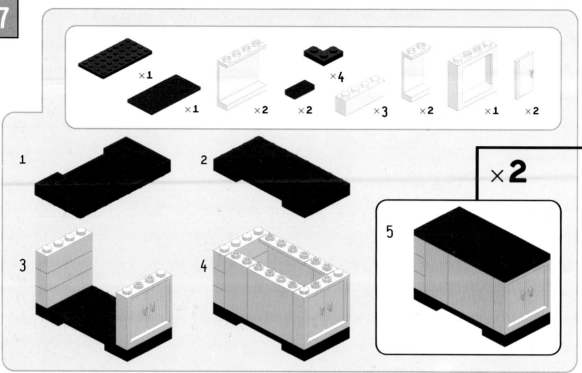

× **2**

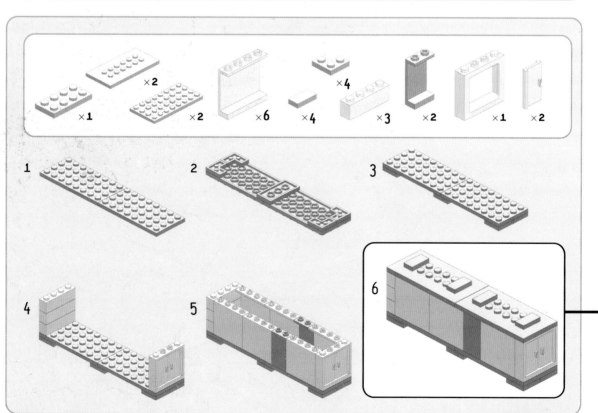

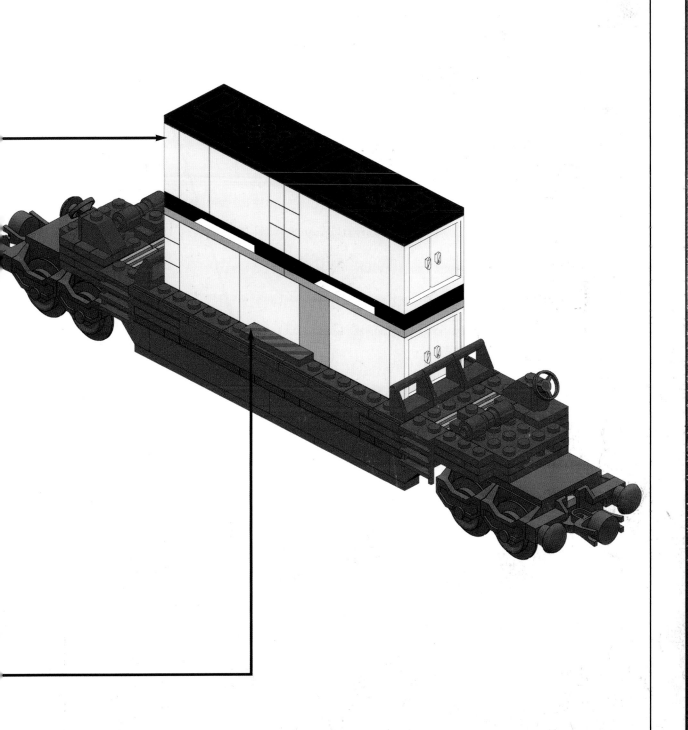

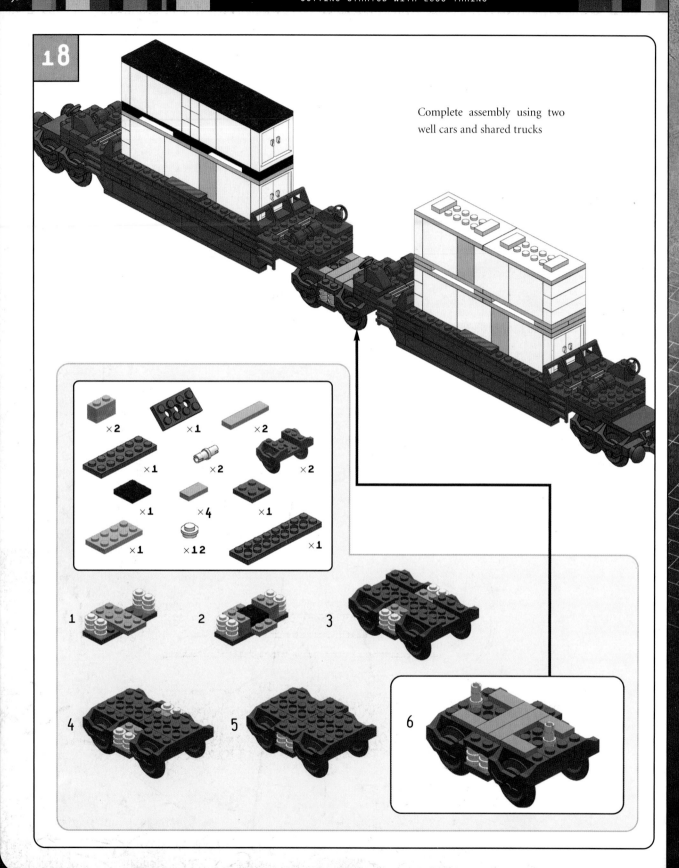

18

Complete assembly using two well cars and shared trucks

CHAPTER 7

TRACK LAYOUTS

What would your own custom-designed LEGO cars be without your own custom-designed track? Just as you can design your own LEGO Train cars, you can create an unlimited variety of designs with your track, from a small oval in the middle of your living room floor to a huge basement layout, or anything in between.

BASIC LAYOUTS

The following are just a few track layouts to help you get started. Of course, like all LEGO themes, the possibilities are limitless. Begin with these layouts, and then develop your own.

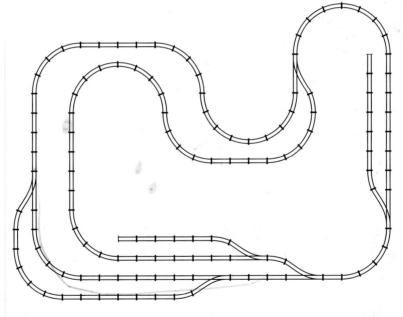

58 STRAIGHT TRACK
46 CURVE TRACK
3 LEFT HAND SWITCH
3 RIGHT HAND SWITCH

This is a monster layout, but great fun. You need plenty of room to set this one up, though.

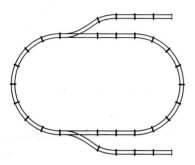

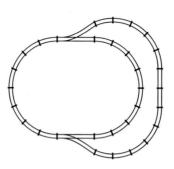

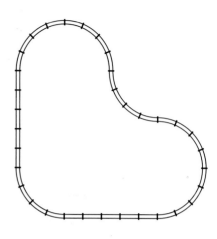

10 STRAIGHT TRACK

16 CURVE TRACK

1 LEFT HAND SWITCH

1 RIGHT HAND SWITCH

This is nice to build as your first layout. You can even use the branches to set aside extra train cars and locomotives.

2 STRAIGHT TRACK

26 CURVE TRACK

1 LEFT HAND SWITCH

1 RIGHT HAND SWITCH

This is a good layout if you've got a bunch of extra curved track. Notice that there are only two straights.

10 STRAIGHT TRACK

24 CURVE TRACK

This layout is very useful if you want to cover a good distance in a relatively small area, or if you want to test a new train on curves and straights.

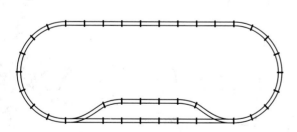

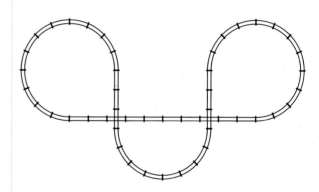

17 STRAIGHT TRACK

18 CURVE TRACK

1 LEFT HAND SWITCH

1 RIGHT HAND SWITCH

12 STRAIGHT TRACK

32 CURVE TRACK

2 CROSS TRACKS

This layout looks like everyone's favorite mouse.

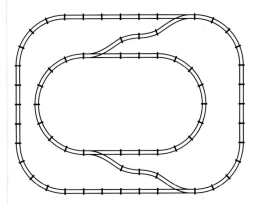

22 STRAIGHT TRACK

36 CURVE TRACK

2 LEFT HAND SWITCH

2 RIGHT HAND SWITCH

A full curve inside the larger outside loops makes this layout great fun.

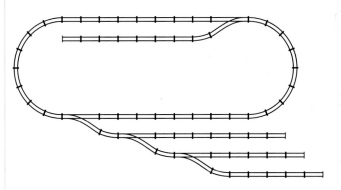

40 STRAIGHT TRACK

20 CURVE TRACK

1 LEFT HAND SWITCH

3 RIGHT HAND SWITCH

This layout is similar to real life train yards, with several spur tracks for "parking" your train cars.

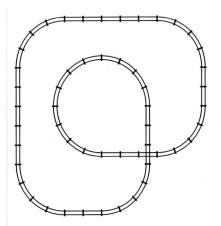

18 STRAIGHT TRACK

32 CURVE TRACK

1 CROSS TRACK

A fun layout for a small space.

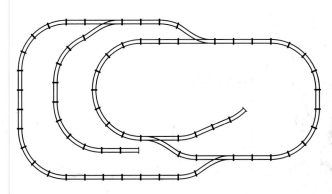

23 STRAIGHT TRACK

36 CURVE TRACK

2 LEFT HAND SWITCH

2 RIGHT HAND SWITCH

It's always fun to build big layouts, and this is a great one.

→ **NOTE**: *For more track layout inspiration, please refer to the accompanying Web site for this book: www.bricksonthebrain/ trains.*

When laying out your track, be sure to set it up on a flat, stable surface. It is best to create your layouts on a large table, or a concrete, linoleum, tile, or hardwood floor. Carpeted floors are usable, but they can cause the track to flex up and down due to variations in the carpet height. Any flex in the track can cause your trains to derail. For instance, if you run

the track from a carpet to a tile floor, the height difference will bend the track. When train cars hit this bend, they may jump off the tracks. Stick to a single height for now.

→ **NOTE**: *Later in this chapter, I will discuss ways to change the height or elevation of your track.*

TIPS AND TRICKS FOR LEGO TRAINS
Setting up and running your LEGO Trains and train track is pretty easy, but here are a few helpful tips to make the process even easier.

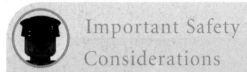

Important Safety Considerations

LEGO TRAINS ARE FOR INDOOR USE ONLY.

DO NOT EXPOSE ELECTRICAL COMPONENTS TO WATER, MOISTURE, OR OPERATE IN ANY DAMP AREA.

DO NOT DISASSEMBLE ELECTRICAL COMPONENTS. THERE ARE NO USER-SERVICEABLE PARTS INSIDE.

DO NOT OPERATE THE POWER UNIT IF THE CORD IS DAMAGED OR IF THE TRANSFORMER OR SPEED REGULATOR IS BROKEN.

IF THE TRANSFORMER SHOWS ANY INDICATION OF EXCESSIVE HEATING, DISCONNECT IT FROM THE POWER OUTLET IMMEDIATELY.

USE THE TRANSFORMER AND SPEED REGULATOR ONLY WITH THE LEGO TRAIN SYSTEM. IT IS NOT DESIGNED FOR ANY OTHER USES.

DISCONNECT THE TRANSFORMER FROM THE WALL OUTLET WHEN NOT IN USE.

- Use only one or two train motors on the same track at once. In addition to safety issues, any more than two motors will start to greatly decrease the speed and pulling power of the motors.
- Avoid having the train pull very heavy loads, which can strain the motor and ultimately burn it out.
- Be sure to start long trains *slowly* or the magnetic couplers may pull apart because of the weight of the cars.
- Do not place metal parts on or across tracks.
- LEGO Train motors do not require lubrication.

TRACK MAINTENANCE
The LEGO track system doesn't require regular maintenance, but keeping it ready to run is easy! Here are a few suggestions for keeping it in great shape.

STORING TRACK
When you are not using your track, be sure to store it in a warm, dry place. Do not store it where it might get damp. Moisture will cause the track to oxidize, which will cause performance problems when running your trains.

CLEANING TRACK
Tracks can accumulate dirt or oxidation after extensive use. Use a soft dry cloth to remove dust or other material. If there is a buildup on the rail (oxidation, dirt, or other substances),

use a pencil eraser to "erase" the buildup.

For severe oxidation on the rails, use an oil such as "Contact Clean" that dissolves the oxidation and is designed specifically for electronics. This type of oil is available through local electronics stores, such as Radio Shack. Never use steel wool or similar abrasive cleaners on tracks or other parts. The metal on the rails is very thin and should be treated with respect!

→ **NOTE**: *Electrical parts are not washable, and you should never expose the tracks to water.*

Now that you know how to get started, it's time to build your first LEGO Train layout. Before you continue on to the second part of this book, take some time to set up your layout, build your cars and locomotives, and run your trains.

When you are comfortable running your trains, continue on to the next section where we will focus on several specific projects that will help you get started building your own LEGO Train designs, adding buildings and landscaping to your layout, and making your track layouts even bigger and better!

AVOIDING SHORT CIRCUITS
LEGO Train track layouts are pretty simple to assemble. The most difficult part of creating

train layouts is avoiding short circuits, which stem from problems in the track design. Short circuits occur when the layout has the train changing directions over the same stretch of track. For example, the layout shown here allows the train to go in only one direction. (Figure 1)

However, the *P*-shaped track design shown next is problematic. Look at the point marked on the track design, and then follow it around the curve. You will see that when you reach that same point again, the train will be pointing in the opposite direction — it has changed direction. The train enters the loop, it circles around on itself, and it will exit the loop at the same place it entered. (Figure 2)

These loops are called *reversing loops* — loops where the train passes one point on the track going one direction, and the next time it passes that same point, it is going the opposite direction.

Reversing loops can cause short circuits. If your layout has a short circuit, certain parts of the track layout will short out and lose power.

These two examples are simple enough. But what if you need to check for short circuits on huge layouts? Well, that's a bit more difficult, though certainly not impossible. What is needed is a system.

Here's how to approach this problem. Power flows through the rails in one direction, and if the track is set up correctly, the power just flows around the track in a steady stream. But when power flows around the track and hits itself, a short circuit occurs. To check for short circuits on larger layouts, simply imagine that each rail is a different color. Trace the rails, and if the imagined colors meet on the same track (as shown here), you have a short circuit. (Figure 3)

→ **NOTE**: *The transformer has a built-in switch that will shut the train off if a short circuit occurs. The green light on the speed regulator will dim or turn off if a short circuit occurs.*

LEGO Track Technical Details

LENGTH OF ONE PIECE OF TRACK:

STRAIGHT TRACK: 5.07 INCHES (12.875 CM)

CURVED TRACK: 5.25 INCHES (13.5 CM), 22.5⁰ ARC ANGLE

WIDTH OF ONE PIECE OF TRACK:

FROM CENTER OF RAIL TO CENTER OF RAIL (ALSO KNOWN AS **ON CENTER**): 1.57 INCHES (4 CM)

OUTER EDGE OF RAIL TO OUTER EDGE OF RAIL: 1.69 INCHES (4.3 CM); INNER EDGE OF RAIL TO INNER EDGE OF RAIL: 1.5 INCHES (3.8 CM). THIS MEASURE IS ALSO KNOWN AS THE **GAUGE**.

TOTAL WIDTH OF TRACK INCLUDING THE 2×8 DARK GRAY PLATE UNDER THE RAILS: 2.5 INCHES (6.3 CM)

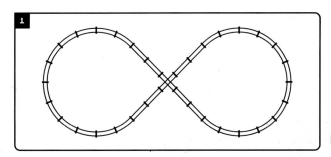

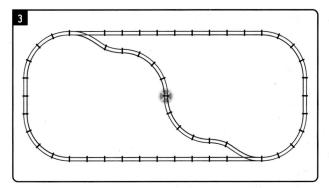

CHANGING TRACK ELEVATION

Flat layouts are great fun, but it's a lot more fun to change the height of the track, or to have one track cross over another. With some basic building techniques, you can easily create bridges, inclines, and more.

Elevation changes, also known as inclines, are best created on a stretch of straight track rather than on curves, because the train motor will have an easier time climbing on straights (and the train motors will last longer). Inclines on curves require slower train speeds and highly stable support structures due to the changing forces as the train rounds the curve.

While you can create an incline on straights or curves, switches are off limits because there is simply no good way to build them. Even if you could figure out a way to create a decent supporting structure, the constant force of using the actual switch to change the active track would cause the support structure to come apart.

→ **NOTE**: *If your incline starts after a switch track section, make sure that there is at least one straight between a switch and the beginning of an incline. This will help ensure that the movement of switching doesn't affect your incline.*

Regardless of how you create an incline, a stable structure to support the track is the key to success, and it is of major importance on curves. You don't want the track to collapse or break apart, sending your newest train creation flying across the floor in a thousand pieces.

→ **NOTE**: *The real key to inclines is not in going up but in coming down. To get up an incline, you can simply add another motor, but when coming down, your train can pick up speed and end up going at a breakneck pace.*

The following steps will guide you through creating inclines that will work quite nicely.

STEP 1: FIGURING OUT THE HEIGHT

Determine how high the incline will be. The amount of incline will be determined by how high and how quickly you want to raise the track.

For example, you might want to simply raise the tracks a small amount to give your train layout the look of a hilly environment. This may require an incline of only 2 – 4 bricks.

Or you may want to build the track high enough to go over another track, allowing another train to pass freely below this track, creating a bridge effect. In order to make sure that most, if not all, trains can pass underneath the bridge, you will need to create the bridge at least 12 bricks high. Of course, some layouts will require more bricks for the height, in order to ensure that all trains can go safely under the bridge. (Figure 4)

STEP 2: CREATING THE SUPPORT COLUMNS

For an incline to be usable, it must have a stable support structure. In this chapter, I will simply use columns, but feel free to use any design style you want.

At first glance, it seems that the obvious way to make an incline is to raise the track by one or two LEGO bricks for every piece of track. Unfortunately, this creates a very steep slope, and only the shortest of trains will be able to make it up this incline. Trains of normal length, and trains going up curved inclines, will either not make it at all or will have trouble getting enough traction to make it all the way. And what's more, trains going downhill on these steep slopes will fly off the track.

The ideal way to create inclines is to create columns that raise the track by only one *plate* per section of track. This will produce a nice gentle incline that even long trains should be able to successfully climb. Of course,

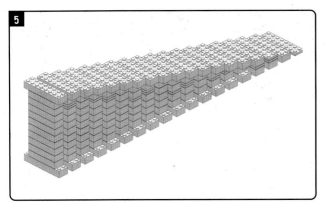

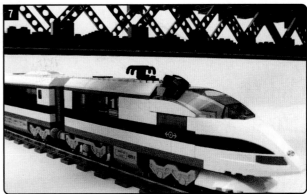

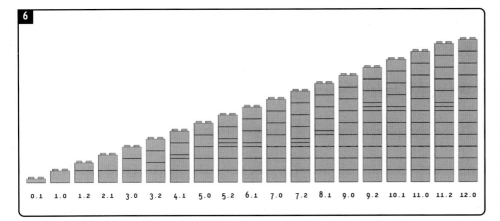

0.1   1.0   1.2   2.1   3.0   3.2   4.1   5.0   5.2   6.1   7.0   7.2   8.1   9.0   9.2   10.1   11.0   11.2   12.0

this means that you will fill your house with train track, because you'll need a lot of space in order to raise the track to any real height.

A better, and more realistic, solution is to raise the track by two plates for each section of track. The above diagram outlines the height of the series of support columns required to reach 12 bricks high — the minimum height to allow another train to pass below. As you can see, it takes 19 columns and 19 sections of track to get to this height. (Figures 5 & 6)

This diagram shows the number of columns required to build an incline to the height of 12 bricks using the two-plate rule. The brick and plate count is represented by a number shown as *brick.plate*. For example, 9.2 means 9 bricks and 2 plates.

You would think that using this two-plate rule, your first column would be two plates high. The initial lead-up to the incline, however, is a little smoother if you start with only one plate for the first column. This will help ease your trains into the incline, making it easy for them to climb. Building from that point, you would continue adding two plates per new column.

When building inclines that lead to a bridge, you can use this concept in reverse. Towards the top of the incline, the last few columns should only change height by one plate, rather than two. This will help to smooth the transition from incline to flat, allowing trains to easily move from the incline to the bridge.

Keep in mind that building a bridge using this two-plate rule will require some room because you'll be using 19 straights up, and 19 down. This creates a *really* long stretch of LEGO track. To reduce the space needed, you can use a curve on the lower parts of the incline, though if you do, your longer trains may have trouble climbing the curved incline.

→ **NOTE**: *If you like long trains and want curved inclines, consider building the incline at one plate per piece of track on the curves. This will help ease the strain on the motor and make it easier for a long train to actually make it to the top of the incline.*

Support columns are great because you can build them to meet your needs and design preferences. The following image shows one possible design style. Feel free to use this style, or better yet, come up with a new style. (Figure 7)

STEP 3: PLACING THE PILLARS UNDER THE TRACK

Snap the track sections together, and then snap the support columns in place under the connections between the tracks. By placing one stud on each piece of the joined track, the support columns will help the track to stay fixed together at its weakest point.

STEP 4: TESTING
THE INCLINE

Once you have built your incline, test it.

First, test your incline with only a locomotive, in case your support columns aren't built sturdily enough. If your support columns fall, you'll know that they're not strong enough, and you'll avoid having derailed train cars all over the floor. Make sure to take the locomotive through the incline at several different speeds.

Next, test the incline with a locomotive and several test train cars to ensure that a full train can make it over the incline. (Don't use your favorite cars in case they go flying off the incline.) Again, test at several speeds.

Finally, try a few different locomotives and train cars. Test longer and longer trains until you find a point where certain trains start to have troubles. Keep that in mind for running the trains later. You wouldn't want to show off your train layout to your friends and not be able to make it over the incline.

INTERVIEW WITH
DAN PARKER ON
TRACK LAYOUTS

Dan Parker has a diverse background ranging from retailing and distribution to engineering R&D and teaching. His personal interests include historical technology, woodworking, industrial design, and model railroading, which, according to Dan, "all stem from and come back together when working in the LEGO medium." Dan recalls that a small Christmas tree layout in 1991 led to cofounding the Pacific Northwest LEGO Train Club in 1997. Dan currently oversees TrainBuilder Productions, LLC and FunBricks, LLC, which provide LEGO-based display events and educational services. He resides in Auburn, Washington, with his wife, Val, and two children, Nathalie and Andrew.

• • •

Jake: It seems like you put on a lot of different types of events. How do you plan a LEGO train layout?

Dan: Track plans are my favorite area of LEGO trains, and usually are the first thing I look at when viewing any train layout.

I start by identifying the purpose of the layout and several important factors. For example, I first consider the nature of the layout. Is the layout something our family would like to quickly set up on the carpet, or am I creating a public exhibition on tables. Generally I like to build the largest layout possible, so I start by looking at resource constraints — time, space, and certainly my collection of track. I may have fixed table sections that must be integrated into the layout or ideas of scenes I'd like to create. If others are participating or I need to get more trains running at once, I'll plan nested loops or a multilevel layout.

Jake: What is the hardest thing for you, when you are setting up LEGO Train layouts?

Dan: Often it's that I simply can't include a certain design element or feature due to space constraints, but this is more on the design end. During actual setup, it's often that other operators have got the jump on me and are already running their trains.

Jake: So I hear that you guys tried to get a Guinness World Records entry for something having to do with LEGO Trains. What was that all about?

Dan: Yes, we wanted to get a world record for the longest LEGO Train layout. There were no constraints here, as the area was 3,500 square feet. We pulled in track from LEGO Enthusiasts around North America and with support of the the LEGO Company. Following the process I talked about earlier, and with a lot of input, we established several areas of the layout: city, town, European, wild west, space, a 100 foot waterway, areas for creations built by the public, and much more. Then I added many types of individual loops (folded dogbones, concentrics, etc.), elevated lines, and specialty circuits. The key was the ability to make discrete "cuts" to convert this from a single, 3,343 foot noodle to the 33 circuits once we achieved the record.

Jake: So, did you get the record?

Dan: Yes! With the help of the LEGO #5206 Speed Computer, a train ran the entire length in about 45 minutes. This was witnessed by three judges and thousands of event attendees. I must say that it was a privilege to coordinate the 40 or so LEGO enthusiasts from both the US and Canada to create the layout. Sadly, we never heard from the Guinness committee after submitting our documentation packet.

Jake: What else can you tell us about LEGO track layouts?

Dan: Over the last six years, I've designed 80–90 or more track plans and always with only a pen and paper. It's a fun challenge and often means the chance to get together with others, either to see the latest company set or a custom creation.

APPENDIX A

RAILROAD TERMINOLOGY

MODEL RAILROAD TERMS

BOGIE PLATE A plate that sits on top of the wheels and attaches to the wagon plate (the long plate that is used as the bottom of a box car). The bogie plate enables the box cars to tilt and lean into the curves as they travel along the track.

COUPLER Device that joins one train car to another.

GAUGE The distance between the inside of the heads of track rails. Most real railroads in North America and Europe are built to a standard gauge of 4' 8 ½". Narrow gauge means rails with a smaller gauge than standard gauge.

MAINLINE The main set of train tracks in a particular area. The mainline typically carries a major amount of the overall traffic in an area.

OPERATION Running trains on a layout in a way that simulates real railroad activity.

PROTOTYPE Model railroader term meaning *real-world train*.

SCALE The size of things on a model railroad, relative to things on a real railroad. For example, in the most popular scale, HO, models are 1/87 of full size.

SELECTIVE COMPRESSION A method of modeling where the builder or designer selects the key elements of the real-world design to be used in the model, thus recreating the impression of the real-world version.

SIDING (OR SPUR) An off-shoot track that branches off from the mainline. This is typically where one train will go to let another pass by in the opposite direction.

TRAIN BASE PLATE This is the base plate that most official LEGO Trains are built on. This base plate comes in two sizes: 6×24 or 6×28.

UNDERCARRIAGE A term that refers to the equipment on the underside of a train car.

VOLTAGE The amount of electric power that is used. The current standard for LEGO Trains is 9 volt power.

PROTOTYPE RAILROAD TERMS

BALLAST A layer of crushed rock placed on the roadbed to keep the track aligned and allow drainage.

CONSIST The cars that make up a train; also a list of those cars. *Locomotive consist* is a group of engines put together to pull a train.

CROSSOVER Two turnouts and a connecting track that allow a train to be diverted to a parallel track.

EOT DEVICE The end-of-train device (sometimes called a FRED, or flashing rear-end device) that has replaced cabooses. Along with a flashing light, many EOTs can transmit information on brake-line pressure and speed to the locomotive.

GONDOLA A long, flat, open car with short sides for hauling items like iron, steel, and scrap.

HOPPER CAR An open-top car for hauling items that don't need protection, like coal and gravel. These cars are unloaded through doors in funnel-like bins in the bottom of the car. Covered hoppers have roofs and are used to carry grain and other items that need protection from weather.

INTERMODAL Shipments that are carried by more than one mode of transportation, mainly including containers and piggyback trailers.

MOW Maintenance-of-way equipment. This equipment is used by a railroad to keep the track and roadbed in good condition.

REEFER A refrigerator car. These are similar in appearance to boxcars but they have ice or mechanical cooling equipment to refrigerate the cargo.

ROADBED The foundation of built-up earth under the tracks.

ROLLING STOCK Freight and passenger cars.

RUNNING BOARD The walkway along the roof or sides of tank cars.

TRUCK An assembly holding a group of two or more wheelsets together beneath a car.

WHEELSET A pair of wheels connected by an axle.

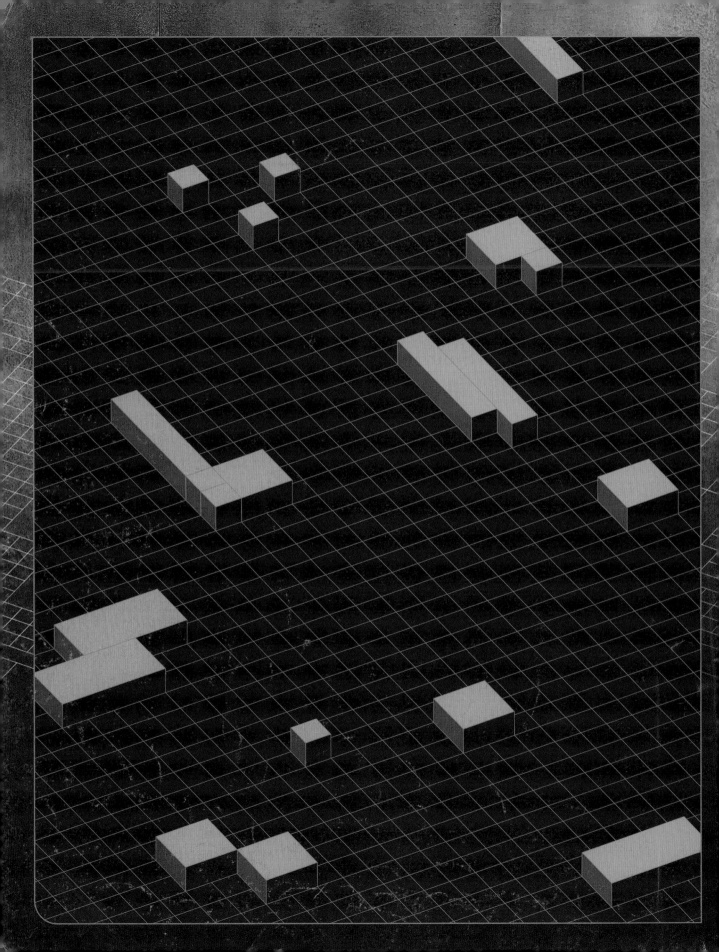

APPENDIX B

WHERE TO BUY LEGO TRAINS

An important part of building LEGO models is finding all the parts you need! Finding the right parts is almost as challenging as designing the models.

PEERON INVENTORIES

WWW.PEERON.COM/INV

Peeron is a great source for finding out which parts are in which sets. Community members have created inventories of most of the LEGO sets. You can search for parts by description or LDraw number. You can also search by set number to get a list of parts in that set.

LEGO SHOP AT HOME

WWW.LEGOSHOP.COM

This is the official direct-sales Web site of the LEGO Company. All current sets are available here, as well as bulk brick packs. This site sometimes offers older or discontinued sets as they pop up in the LEGO warehouses on occasion. The prices on sets at this online store is based on standard retail pricing, but there are Web specials for certain items or groups of items.

PITSCO

WWW.PLDSTORE.COM

Pitsco is the official distributor of LEGO Dacta educational products. In addition to a number of Mindstorms and other robotics products, Pitsco offers a number of great bulk parts packs.

BRICKLINK

WWW.BRICKLINK.COM

Run by LEGO fans, for LEGO fans, BrickLink is a huge virtual mall. Fans can set up a storefront to sell their extra LEGO parts, sets, and other LEGO merchandise. Several million parts are for sale at any one time. If you can't find the parts you need at BrickLink, you'd better just redesign your model!

EBAY

WWW.EBAY.COM

If you have time to wait, eBay can be a great place to find large lots of parts. There are a great many LEGO part auctions on eBay at any one time, but it is sometimes hard to find the exact parts you are looking for. If you are looking for auctions in other parts of the world, the www.eBay.com home page has a list of local version of their site to choose from.

Finding LEGO Parts

WHEN SEARCHING FOR PARTS TO BUILD A DESIGN, YOU MAY FIND THAT YOU CAN'T GET CERTAIN PARTS IN CERTAIN COLORS. SOMETIMES YOU CAN SOLVE THIS PROBLEM BY REPLACING THE PARTICULAR PART WITH A SIMILAR PART. FOR INSTANCE, THE LOCOMOTIVE WE BUILT EARLIER IN THE BOOK USES SEVERAL 1X2X2 WINDOWS—TWO WINDOWS SIDE BY SIDE. IF YOU HAVE TROUBLE FINDING THESE WINDOWS, YOU COULD REPLACE THE SET OF TWO 1 X 2 X 2 WINDOWS WITH ONE 1X2X4 WINDOW.

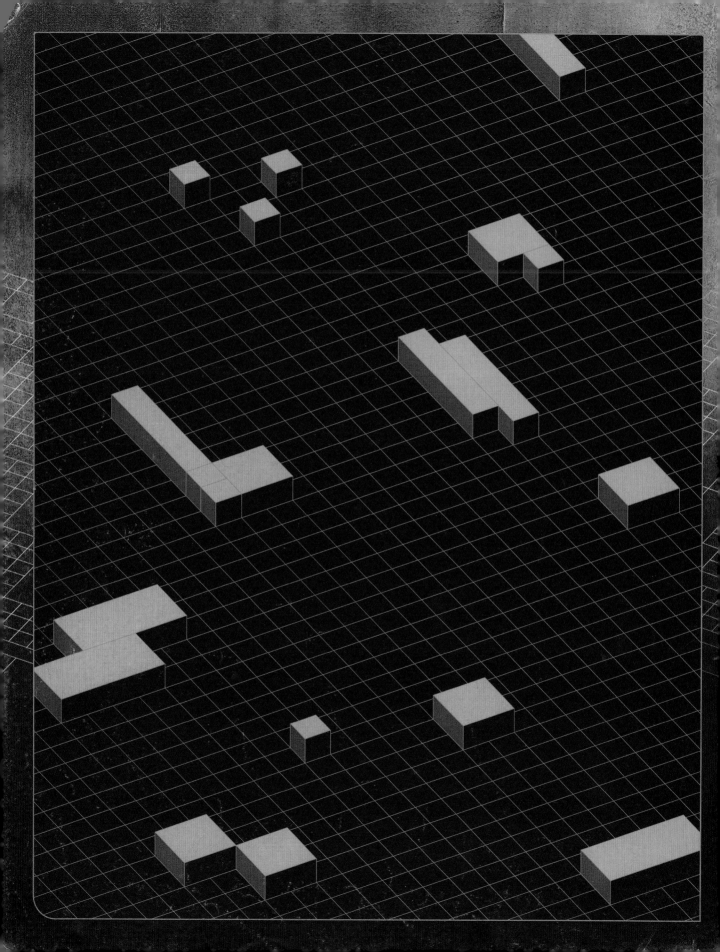

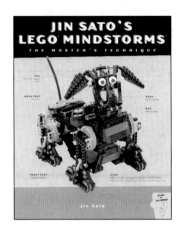